"*No more excuses. Stewart and Tsao have provided a guide to fixing the most common and persistent problems with meetings. The next time you're sitting there feeling like your time is being wasted, throw your copy of Momentum on the table and shout, 'Let's do something about our meetings. The answers are here; we just have to try them!' What have you got to lose? Stewart and Tsao have done the hard work of developing the solution to your meeting problems. The rest is up to you.*"

—BILL PASMORE, PHD, PROFESSOR OF PRACTICE
AT COLUMBIA UNIVERSITY, AUTHOR OF
LEADING CONTINUOUS CHANGE

"*In Momentum: Creating Effective, Engaging & Enjoyable Meetings, Stewart and Tsao provide a thorough guide showing both experienced and developing leaders the core elements for designing and leading meetings that will be effective and will avoid the 'death by meeting' habits we have all learned to hate. A great resource for leaders in every type of organization!*"

—PAUL WHITE, PHD, AUTHOR OF *THE VIBRANT WORKPLACE, THE 5 LANGUAGES OF APPRECIATION IN THE WORKPLACE*, AND OTHERS

"*Momentum is the real deal. Mamie and Tai understand the challenge with meetings goes beyond setting an agenda; it's about the behaviors and mindsets of the people who schedule, lead, and attend them. The authors care deeply about positive interactions and the people behind them, and bring their expertise and experience to an important topic for anyone who works with others.*"

—LINDSEY CAPLAN, DIRECTOR OF TALENT DEVELOPMENT

"*Every small business owner's number one issue is they don't have enough time. Most of their time is spent in meetings and most of those meetings are totally ineffective. This book is such a great resource to business owners for learning how to run better and shorter meetings that create results.*"

—CARISSA REINIGER, FOUNDER & CEO OF SILVER LINING, AUTHOR OF *INSPIRING ENTREPRENEURS*

Creating Effective,
Engaging, and
Enjoyable Meetings

Momentum

Mamie Kanfer Stewart
and Tai Tsao

LIONCREST
PUBLISHING

www.meeteor.com
www.mamieks.com
www.taitsao.com

MOMENTUM

Creating Effective, Engaging and Enjoyable Meetings

ISBN   978-1-61961-725-4 *Paperback*
          978-1-61961-726-1 *Ebook*

To the unsung heroes of effective meetings.

Contents

Introduction

_____

For decades, a problem capable of destroying productivity and crushing morale has plagued the business community. It impacts almost everyone in an operation, from the highest executive to the newest hire. If you're reading this book, chances are you've experienced its effects firsthand. Most people have.

Anyone who has ever worked in a professional environment has attended a poorly run meeting.

The scope of the problem is enormous. According to academic and industry research, the amount of time Americans spend in meetings every week is staggering. Professor Steven Rogelberg of the University of North Carolina, along with his fellow researchers, cited in *The Cambridge Handbook of Meeting Science*, that on average, employees spend 6 hours and managers spend more than 23 hours a week in meetings. The number keeps growing. According to a study by the late Joseph Allen, professor at the University of Nebraska at Omaha, over one-third of meetings are unnecessary. For some managers, this equates to up to 8 hours of lost productivity each week. That translates into thousands of dollars lost. Across America, it's a multibillion-dollar problem.

As widespread as the issue is, few organization leaders are taking it seriously and doing something to actively address it. As businesses become more dispersed geographically, they also become more complex internally. Virtual and cross-functional teams only exacerbate the problem when, instead, meetings should play an even more important role in keeping everyone connected and committed to a shared vision. How a company responds to this challenge is a key component of its culture.

It's time to take meetings more seriously. They are a critical and fundamental component to how work gets done. We know through research and firsthand experience that effective collaboration enhances creativity and yields greater results. Working together produces synergy that enables us to accomplish more together than any of us can alone. In other words, meetings are here to stay.

As professionals, we spend an inordinate amount of time in meetings, but few of us are trained on how to maximize their benefits. Training employees to effectively lead, manage, and engage in meetings is not on most companies' professional development agendas. Some organizations might offer facilitation training for managers or agenda templates, but most lack a systematic approach for educating employees on how to run effective meetings. Even business school students are not taught how to run meetings, despite the fact many will spend a third of their working hours in them.

Our use of technology to help enhance the meeting experience is greatly lacking as well. The scheduling tools we all rely upon to "plan" meetings don't facilitate the creation of a thoughtful agenda, or any agenda for that matter. We're often consumed by the logistical challenges and therefore overlook the role technology can play as a tool to support productive meeting habits.

This book will provide you with a start-to-finish guide for running successful, productive, worthwhile meetings. Its contents come from extensive research conducted on the subject, as well as our own personal, widely diverse experiences in the business world. Through our work with Meeteor, we've heard from hundreds of people about their best and worst meetings and identified highly common and obscure practices—both good and bad.

MAMIE'S STORY

"Have a productive day," my dad would call as he ran out the door each morning on his way to work. From a young age, I was driven to make things better—more effective, more efficient, more enjoyable. I started my first business at age twelve, when I decided I could run a better summer camp than the one I'd attended for the past two years. The experience crystallized my passion for making something better in a way that benefits others—a passion that still drives me today.

Several years ago, I found my true mission: enabling others to work in ways that make them happier and more impactful. I decided to devote my career to helping businesses improve efficiency, boost morale, and generally run better. I launched a company, Meeteor, and while it started out addressing several business needs, the focus soon centered on meetings.

Once I began speaking with people about meetings, it was clear bad meetings were a widespread issue in desperate need of a solution. I'd walk into a networking event, tell someone I started a business to improve meetings, and, like clockwork, they'd light up and launch into the story of their latest meeting debacle. Every single person described a horrible meeting experience, many of which happened earlier that day or week. It was clear we were onto something. I wasn't the only one who saw meetings as a real problem that existed everywhere, and people were ready for a change.

I never had formal training in meetings or project management. I learned effective ways of working from direct experience. Shortly after I graduated from college, I began working in my family's enterprise, GOJO Industries, a global leader in hygiene and skin health and the inventor of PURELL® Instant Hand Sanitizer. My great-aunt and uncle, Goldie and Jerry Lippman, founded GOJO in 1946. Goldie passed away before I was born, but Jerry was like a grandfather to me and my siblings, and we called him "Grandpa Jerry."

Back in the 1940s, Goldie Lippman—like many women during World War II—worked on the manufacturing floor of an Akron, Ohio, rubber company. There she discovered how difficult it was to clean her hands after a day's work. Chemical cleaners were available, but the graphite, carbon, and tar on her skin required the use of harsh agents like benzene to be removed. That took a toll on workers' hands, and Jerry, who completed only tenth grade but loved to tinker and experiment, set out to find a better solution. Walking the halls of Kent State University, Jerry found chemistry Professor Clarence Cook to consult with on the invention of the first heavy-duty, waterless hand cleaner, which could be used safely and effectively to remove heavy soils away from a sink. Grandpa Jerry mixed the new hand cleaner in his mother-in-law's basement washing machine and sold it from out of the back of his car.

Over time, GOJO experienced continued growth and created a full portfolio of market-specific, science-based hygiene and skin health solutions for industrial settings, restaurants, offices, and other professional environments. GOJO launched many other new products, including the first portion-controlled soap dispenser. Building on decades of innovation, in the late 1980s, GOJO invented PURELL® Hand Sanitizer. This new product provided a safe and effective solution for hand hygiene away from the sink. It was a breakthrough in healthcare, where healthcare professionals, who wash their hands one hundred times or more per day, benefited dramatically from a solution that was effective and much gentler on their skin than soap and water. PURELL® Hand Sanitizer was a logical next step for an innovative company that started out solving real human problems with science and technology.

In 2007, the company declared a GOJO Purpose—Saving Lives and Making Life Better through Well-Being Solutions. This Purpose builds on its foundational history and, today, galvanizes the organization to advance health and well-being. To achieve this, the GOJO team became inspired to collaborate in a complex, growing organization, which required them to work together in new ways, drawing upon leading-edge management theories and redesigning its practices and tools. As a result, GOJO created a professionally managed entrepreneurial enterprise, which is one of the keys to its ongoing success.

These ways of working spread from GOJO into our family

office and family philanthropies. When I began working as the first professional staff member for our family foundation in 2005, these successful practices had long been in place. No one explicitly spoke about them; it was simply how everyone worked. As a recent college graduate with an art degree, I had minimal organizational office experience. I worked closely with many experienced professionals to learn how to create meetings where everyone was engaged and the time was worthwhile. I learned how to plan and organize an agenda. They taught me the importance of taking good notes, which I soon learned is not just an administrative task. I came to understand the importance of shared, effective processes and supporting tools and templates, and how, together, they create a thriving work environment where meetings elevate everything from productivity to morale.

After a while, my position at the foundation morphed into a consulting role. I'd work with grantees on strategic planning, staffing, and governance work—all processes I'd learned from people at GOJO. As a consultant, I loved working with people to build their individual and organizational capacity. Unlike most consultants, in addition to facilitating the process that resulted in a strategic plan or hiring a new staff member, I'd also teach my clients the new practices so they could continue to do this work without me. However, once my work on these projects was done, I wasn't leaving the teams with much more than some PowerPoint slides and a few Word templates to guide them in my absence.

Today at Meeteor, we combine leading, cutting-edge thinking on team collaboration with best practices from real-life experiences from GOJO, and others, to help clients incorporate these techniques into their own organizations. Our practices are derived and supported by research and academic analysis, with a foundation in the tools and processes that hundreds of GOJO teams have employed over the last two decades.

Meeteor is a collaboration company on a mission to build strong, healthy teams in which people thrive and organizations succeed. Since our founding in 2013, we've offered a variety of products and services to support effective meetings and teamwork, including web and mobile apps, trainings, consulting, coaching, and resource publication. We know changing behavior is a complicated process, and we continually learn from our customers and evolve our offerings to best serve teams and organizations as they adopt and sustain effective practices around meetings.

TAI'S STORY

From the outset, Mamie understood that behavioral change is both difficult and the foundation of productivity. To succeed, she knew Meeteor needed someone who understood this complex subject. In search of the right person, she reached out to a friend of mine, a fellow Columbia graduate, and we connected through her. I was immediately drawn to Mamie's vision for Meeteor, as it closely aligns with my personal mission—to help individuals, teams, and organizations unlock their potential, transform the way they work, and make a greater impact.

My background is in organizational development and management consulting. Meeting best practices have been part of my job from the very beginning of my career—I live and breathe them. I was very fortunate to have had the opportunity to learn from a talented group of leaders and mentors.

The first leader I worked closely with, David Tai, has been a great influence on me. I worked with David at the management consulting firm he founded in Taiwan, where I was born and raised. David worked for IBM for twenty years before starting his own company. IBM is known for its business process, structure, and professional development, and David implemented many of the great meeting practices at our consulting firm. These meeting best practices, many of them similar to GOJO's, not only support a positive team culture, but also lead to high levels of client engagement.

We regularly heard positive feedback from our clients on how the meetings we ran helped move things forward and how much they appreciate the thoughtfulness we put into them. We facilitated meetings with many executives in our client organizations with the understanding their time is very precious. We needed to make sure every conversation was meaningful and led to tangible outcomes and actionable next steps. Our meeting notes drove actions and moved the projects forward. These practices are especially helpful when working with external clients and customers. I was fortunate to have worked at a company that champions effective meeting practices and whose leaders model the behaviors at every moment. I started asking myself how I could recreate this positive work culture for more people.

Helping others become more successful was not something new to me. Almost a decade ago, I founded i Talent Learning community, a nonprofit organization, to guide college students in becoming self-directed learners and to develop their core competence to become future leaders. Many students didn't know what they were going to do after graduation, and everyone was confused about career development. I, along with other mentors, designed programs such as real-world projects and interactive workshops to help these aspiring future leaders learn and apply the key skills to help them launch and sustain successful careers. One of the first fundamental skills we teach is how to run effective meetings.

For these young talents, teamwork is not a new thing, but knowing how to plan, run, and follow through on meetings can be a big differentiator in their careers and leadership journeys. Some business professionals are never trained how to run meetings in their careers. Those who are trained typically only learn how to run meetings after they are promoted to management, years into their career. Even then, many of them follow standards set by their predecessors and coworkers, regardless of their effectiveness. When these young talents know how to best prepare for meetings, contribute their thoughts, and capture effective meeting notes, they stand out from their peers and facilitate collaboration without authority. Years later, I still hear wonderful stories from the students we worked with about their best meeting moments and how the skills and mindset prepared them for their career wins.

I later came to the United States to further my learning and diversify my experience in the field of organization development, organizational change, and learning, and received my master's degree in Social-Organizational Psychology at Columbia University. I enjoy helping teams across different industries—from businesses, nonprofit organizations, and government agencies to higher education institutes—reflect on how they work with each other and learn about how effective meeting practices can improve their collaboration. I apply group dynamics, behavioral science, human-centered design, and learning theories to my work at Meeteor.

We're devoted to introducing new ways of working and helping people integrate them with their daily work. We believe no matter where you're at in your career, whether you've learned from inspirational leaders or mentors, or have worked at an organization that champions thoughtful process, you have the potential to make these effective meeting practices your own. You'll have the confidence to plan thoughtful agendas, facilitate meaningful conversations, and capture meeting notes that drive actions. Moreover, by applying these meeting practices, you'll help shape the culture of your team, your organization, and the people you work with. That's our dream and we're here to help you succeed.

HOW THIS BOOK CAN HELP YOU

Despite its prevalence in the workplace, the problem of unproductive meetings has not yet been adequately addressed. Though academic research on meetings and their effectiveness began a few decades ago, only recently have researchers started to consolidate modern knowledge on the science of meeting-related activities. It's similar in the practitioner world. It's been almost fourteen years since renowned business author Patrick Lencioni published *Death by Meeting*, a critical piece of literature that points out the problem of meetings in the business world.

Compared to other similar collaborative business practices, such as task management and customer relationship management, meeting management is still in its infancy. Even with an increasing number of articles being published in the *Harvard Business Review*, the *New York Times*, and other publications, there still are not enough businesses devoted to helping organizations create strong, healthy meeting cultures. There is a dearth of trainings on how to have productive meetings.

The handful of books that do exist on the topic only seem to scratch the surface of the problem and fall short of a nuts-and-bolts, start-to-finish action guide to transforming meeting cultures. While most promote useful models and worthwhile practices, they are designed more like reference guides, lacking information on how to apply practices in real life. There is no consideration for the human dynamics at play.

Real behavior change requires much more than simply introducing a concept to the reader. To provide this, we've created a start-to-finish look at what makes meetings work, what makes them fail, what role technology should play, and ways to make sure your experiences moving forward are productive and positive.

We work to educate clients and support the changes they're implementing every day. We do this through our products, coaching, consulting, and trainings. This book is a guide any manager, leader, or meeting participant can use to implement our process daily, in real-life work. No matter where you are, what size company you're in, or how long you've been in the workforce, the approaches and tools detailed here can work for you.

This book will help you understand how meetings cost your organization, both financially and psychologically, and how successful meetings can make any business more agile, faster, and more productive in the long run. It will show you how to imbed this mentality into the DNA of your culture. It will lay out the anatomy of a successful meeting and tell you everything you should be doing before, during, and after. It will illuminate different practices for meeting leaders and participants, address the most common meeting challenges and how to overcome them, provide examples, and recommend next steps so you can immediately put your learnings into action.

Most importantly, this book will teach you how to achieve results.

We encourage you to make this book work for you and your team's specific needs and culture. You might find some practices to be absolute miracles and others that will never fly. As you encounter new approaches, recognize your own biases. For some, this will mean making an extra effort to keep an open mind and attempting to talk to your team members or manager about implementing new practices that may feel awkward. For others, this will mean containing your excitement and potentially taking baby steps, even though you know much more is necessary. Over time, the goal is to expand your influence so many more feel the urgency and drive to transform their meetings, ultimately creating a deep and sustained impact within your organization.

At times, we will share our personal stories to help bring the concepts to life. Our stories will span industries and sectors, our roles in the organizations and meetings, and meeting types. In some cases, we will describe situations we've witnessed or heard from our customers and peers in the business community. Throughout the book, we'll tell our stories as one voice using the first person singular point of view.

HOW TO USE THIS BOOK

This book will give you a blueprint and tool kit. You don't have to read it cover-to-cover, nor do you have to read it in order. At the end of each chapter, there will be a bullet point chapter review with key takeaways to highlight and reinforce the learnings and act as a quick reference guide.

We wrote this book to inspire actions, so you will also find an action list at the end of each chapter with specific steps to help you crystallize the learnings and implement them in your daily work. We include extensive examples, sample language, guides, and templates to support your action. Some of these are presented within the context of the chapter. You can find others in the resource section at the end of this book or at www.meeteor. com/momentum/resources.

You can read this book alone and implement the practices on your own. Or, you can read this book alongside your colleagues for a more powerful experience. Meetings are not a one-person activity, so why not make transforming your meeting practices a team activity? You can use the first two chapters to reflect on your meeting culture and create an awareness among your team.

Chapters Three and Four explore the root causes of meeting problems and the benefits of meetings. Chapter Five lays out the reasons for running meetings and alternatives to meetings. Chapters Six through Twelve describe the key components of effective meetings and what to do before, during, and after a meeting. Chapter Thirteen highlights additional tips for virtual meetings and how to use technology effectively. Chapter Fourteen discusses how to get buy-in from your team and introduce changes for your meetings. At the end of the book, you'll also find some templates and additional examples to help you put your learnings into action.

The purpose of this book is to give you the knowledge and

support necessary to immediately change your personal ways of working, as well as your team's, and, we hope, your entire organization's. If at any time you have questions this book doesn't address, or you have personal meeting stories and practices you'd like to share, please contact us at book@meeteor.com. We also mention additional resources at various points. You can find examples, templates, and more at www.meeteor.com/momentum/resources.

We truly believe meetings should create momentum that moves your work forward. When people leave a meeting, they should be energized and ready to put the outputs into action. Too many meetings—especially poorly run ones—stop work in its tracks, but this no longer has to be a fact everyone simply accepts. Regardless of your organization, team, or role, you have the power to create meetings that build momentum.

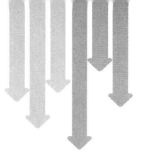

Chapter One

What's the Problem with Meetings?

No one is immune to a bad meeting experience. Just about everyone can come up with their own cringe-inducing story at the mere mention of the topic.

For me, a memorable rough moment happened during one of my nonprofit board meetings. Usually, these meetings are enjoyable and productive. The senior staff is top notch and the board is composed of highly successful businessmen and women who are leaders and experts in their fields. When we all get together, good work gets done.

This particular meeting, however, took a nosedive when a new staff member, let's call her Robin, launched into her allotted time in our two-day agenda. She started by reviewing the pre-meeting materials line by line—the very same materials every single person in that room had already read.

Obviously, Robin was not accustomed to board members coming to meetings prepared. In her defense, it's common in many organizations for meeting participants not to dutifully complete the required pre-reading. However, that is not the case with this board. I even once complained that 65 pages of pre-reading for a 2-day board retreat was excessive in my opinion, but I and every board member still read every page.

As soon as Robin started talking, it was as if someone held up a giant vacuum and magically sucked all the energy out of the room. Within seconds, we all realized we were doomed to what was likely going to be a very long hour.

As she went on and on, I kept looking at the board chair and executive director, wondering why on earth they were allowing this to happen.

It went on for *45 minutes*.

It was torture.

So why didn't I intervene? Because I thought it was not my place. I knew I couldn't be alone in my thinking, but if the board chair and executive director weren't stepping in, I assumed they had a good reason.

As soon as we had a break, I approached the executive director to ask about Robin's portion. She explained she didn't want to deflate Robin during her first meeting with the board. Unfortunately, exactly the opposite happened. We were all frustrated by the wasteful 45 minutes during which no one other than Robin spoke—almost no new information was shared, and nothing moved forward.

In that moment, I realized we all have an obligation to facilitate. I should have said, "Robin, I appreciate you going through this report, as it has a lot of good information, but let's just do a quick check-in. Has everyone here read this?" Everyone would have raised their hands, and I would have replied with, "Great! So what new information did you want to share or what questions do you have for us?" We would have skipped ahead to the discussion portion and a precious near-hour of all our lives would have been saved. More importantly, we would have had a valuable conversation that supported the work of the organization.

People sit through terrible meetings all the time because they don't feel they can do anything about it. Even when they try to intervene, the fear of confrontation and negative group dynamics can hinder their actions. I say it's time for all of us to step in. It's time to address the common factors contributing to this widespread problem of unproductive meetings and put an end to them, once and for all.

WHAT EXACTLY IS A MEETING?

Before diving in, let's define exactly what a "meeting" is. "Meeting" is a broad term that applies to the gathering of 2 or more people. There are many types of meetings, ranging from coffee dates to working sessions, sales calls to board retreats, one-on-ones to conferences, and more. For this book, we'll be focusing on meetings as a time when people, often colleagues or peers, come together to do purposeful work. No matter how it takes place—whether it be in a conference room, over the phone, through Zoom or Skype, or via any other format—the shared goal is to achieve an outcome such as making a decision or enriching an idea.

Email and chat communications, however, are not meetings. While they are important and can be fruitful, they don't require synchronous participation of multiple people.

There are formal and informal meetings. Formal meetings

are scheduled ahead of time. Typically, they are set to discuss something specific with a certain group of people. Informal meetings happen much more frequently and often without us noticing. They occur every time you grab someone to ask a quick question or gather input. They happen when you are standing in the hallway talking about something work related and end up coming to a decision. They are not planned, but they count.

No matter the type of meeting, it runs the risk of being bad and wasting time.

WHAT GOES WRONG?

In my work with business professionals, I have heard it all when it comes to meetings—the good, the bad, and everything in between. Let's delve into "the bad" and examine some of the more common complaints.

"I FIND MYSELF ASKING WHY WE ARE EVEN HAVING THIS MEETING."

This gripe is, by far, the one I hear most. You are in a meeting and the leader dives into the first topic. You almost instantly begin questioning, "Why are we discussing this? Why are we even having this meeting? Why am I here?" Without a clear idea of what the group needs to accomplish, it's almost impossible to understand how this meeting will propel you and your work forward, making the remainder of the meeting feel more like a waste of time than a valuable collaboration.

The same feeling can arise as the meeting comes to an end. You walk out the door wondering why you just spent the last hour discussing the market research study instead of getting three things marked off your to-do list. Sure, the study was interesting, but so what? You find yourself asking, "Did we really need that meeting? Did I really need to be *in* that meeting? And what am I supposed to do now? Did this meeting change anything?"

In both cases, the frustration is palpable. Too many meetings lack a clear purpose that justifies spending our precious time in them.

"MEETINGS ARE A DISTRACTION FROM MY REAL WORK."

Many people consider meetings to be a separate activity from their actual work. Rather than a crucial form of collaboration that helps to accomplish a goal, meetings are seen as a wasteful activity that interferes with productivity. According to a 2017 study conducted by scholars at Harvard Business School, among all the senior managers across different industries who participated in the study, 65 percent said meetings keep them from completing their individual work.

Poorly run meetings are a distraction. They can add to stress levels and inhibit you from getting your actual work done. If you spend your time in unproductive and unnecessary meetings, it can make you feel anxious and steal your attention. This becomes a negative cycle, because you struggle to focus in the meetings, then lack the energy to focus on your work. It's a constant battle.

"MY DAY IS RUN BY MY CALENDAR."

These are the people who are literally in back-to-back meetings all day long. For some, this is a badge of honor. They attach a false sense of self-worth to meetings. As you move up the hierarchy, you start going to more and more meetings. You start to believe that the more meetings you go to, the more important you are. This just isn't true.

For many others, constantly running from one meeting to the next creates a life of unnecessary stress. When you have too many meetings, the calendar automatically takes precedence over everything else, even your to-do list. When you do nothing else but go to meetings every day from 9 to 5, the only ways to get any individual work done is to work during a meeting, work extra hours early in the morning or late at night, or delegate everything so you have no other work. None of these are good options.

Sitting in meetings all day might keep you busy, but it only creates the illusion you are accomplishing anything. If your participation in meetings is truly worthwhile and the meetings themselves are propelling work forward, then a job filled with meetings is completely appropriate. If, on the other hand, many of your meetings do nothing but pull you away from more pressing responsibilities, you are setting yourself up for a life filled with unnecessary frustration, exhaustion, and stress.

"I FEEL LIKE WE MEET ALL THE TIME."

Some companies jump to have meetings for everything and anything. They have a weekly whole-company meeting and departmental meetings and daily team meetings and standing meetings and one-on-one meetings, not to mention all the project meetings and working sessions and meetings with clients. The list goes on and on. Not only is there no time for anything else, but it can start to feel like any time you have the slightest challenge, you should call a meeting.

A friend of mine shared his frustration with this "need-to-meet" culture in his office. He explained he had recently received a phone call from a colleague seeking help. He listened to the colleague explain the issue for about 5 minutes. When the colleague was done, my friend said, "Great. So, what do you need from me?" The colleague seemed almost taken aback. He considered this question and responded, "Actually, nothing." He had talked himself through the problem, which was great. But my friend wished the colleague would have spent a few minutes thinking through the problem on his own before interrupting someone else. What he really needed was space to process, and that doesn't take two people.

When your go-to method is to approach your colleagues for help, you end up taking unnecessary steps to problem solve. Things don't always have to be so complicated or require so much effort. It's important to allow yourself a chance to work through the problem at hand before possibly making a bigger deal out of it than needed. There are even a few alternatives to meetings that address the need to get input, advice, or approval without the heavy lift of a meeting—we will share information on several options in Chapter Six.

The challenge of recurring meetings is that you don't always have a meaningful reason to gather. I've heard reports of standing meetings that begin with the team leader asking, "So who has something to share today?" followed by an awkward silence that lasts until someone says something to fill it. Recurring meetings are great for holding time on busy calendars and ensuring the group has regular check-ins to stay aligned, but not every standing meeting needs to happen every time. It's important to assess whether there's a reason to meet and not just meet because it's on the calendar.

"THERE'S NO WAY I CAN SAY NO TO A MEETING."

At many companies, the idea of declining a meeting because it's not the best use of your time is unheard of. Rarely do people opt out of meetings, even when they secretly question whether their attendance is really worthwhile. They see a meeting invite and accept by default.

When you're in a position of authority, you must be able to trust your team to meet without you. If you are not in a position of authority, declining a meeting might make you feel as if you are turning down work. You might feel like you are saying no to your boss and worry how that will be perceived.

In reality, most meeting planners don't thoughtfully consider who really needs to be in the meeting, who needs to provide input prior to the meeting, and who only needs to be informed of the meeting outcomes. They just add every possible candidate to the invitee list.

I know of one company that had the practice of inviting all 12 employees in their department to every meeting. The notion that everyone might not need to be there was viewed as crazy. How would people know what was going on? How would they be able to give input if they were not present? I call this "Meeting FOMO," or fear of missing out, which arises when teams lack consistent and transparent information-sharing practices. When the only way to contribute or stay informed is to be in the meeting, of course you can't say no.

"NO ONE COMES PREPARED."

There is almost nothing more frustrating than starting a meeting you've prepared for only to find other participants neglected to do the same. I hear this complaint often, both from meeting leaders and participants. The challenge presented when only some people have prepared is twofold. First, how do you make the most of the time you now have with this group of partially prepared people? Second, how do you make those who did prepare feel appreciated so they'll continue to prepare in the future?

Unfortunately, lack of preparation can quickly become a self-perpetuating cycle. When someone comes unprepared and the first part of the meeting is then spent presenting the pre-reading materials or bringing the offender up to speed, everyone else begins to wonder why they prepared. They ask themselves, "Why should I take 10 minutes to read the memo when it's just going to be reviewed in the meeting anyway?"

The alternative approach of going forward with the meeting as if everyone prepared is not always any better. You risk not getting the best thinking from the group. Those who haven't completed the prework haven't had a chance to process the information, and they don't have the full picture. Yet, the conversation must go on, and, while you might accomplish the meeting's outcome, you likely didn't end up with the best result.

Depending on who and how many people are unprepared, you might be left with no other choice than to cannibalize your meeting time for information sharing, which reduces the time you have for dialogue. This means you either rush through the rest of the agenda or schedule another meeting, neither of which are ideal outcomes.

"MEETINGS BRING OUT THE WORST IN PEOPLE."

There are a few common offenders who can contribute greatly to the awfulness of any meeting. Some people talk too much. Some rehash old problems and love to throw fuel on the fire, instead of acknowledging when the conversation is over. There are the folks who only repeat what other people have already said, taking credit or simply wasting time. Then there are the constant dissenters, interrupters, and know-it-alls.

These behaviors are not individual personality issues. These are behavioral issues. Group dynamics in meetings can trigger or amplify disruptive behaviors. How we act reflects our preferences and our interpretation of the actions of those around us. For example, dominating meeting conversations is often seen as a disruptive behavior, but sometimes it's triggered by the group.

I was once in a meeting with my fellow consultants at a firm where I used to work. We were analyzing the client's issue, and one team member was dominating the conversation. She kept talking and elaborating on her ideas, leaving no room for other people to jump in. While I was still processing my thoughts, she suddenly said to me and another colleague, "Are you still with me? You've been so quiet I'm not sure if you understand or agree with me. I can continue explaining if you want." At that point, I realized my quietness fed her assumption that I had reservations about her ideas and triggered her to fill the silence. Her non-stop talking also reinforced my assumption that she just wanted to dominate the conversation. Neither of us came to the meeting intending to be disruptive or make the other person annoyed or uncomfortable, but that's what happened.

Disruptive behaviors fuel frustration among team members. How your colleagues act in meetings can affect your own emotional state. Each person's behavior has the ability to strengthen or weaken your relationship with them. Do your coworkers make you feel valued and respected? Does your team leader encourage you to speak your mind and others to listen without judgment? Do you appreciate and enjoy the interaction with your colleagues? If not, you might feel negative emotions toward your team members, which can permeate beyond the walls of the meeting. If these behaviors are not addressed, you reinforce them at the expense of the team's morale, engagement, trust, and creativity.

"MEETINGS DON'T LEAD TO ANYTHING."

Some meetings can be deceiving. You leave the meeting feeling really energized after a rich discussion. But then, the worst thing of all happens: nothing. All that great conversation was a waste because there is no follow-through. No one writes down the items requiring action, and no one takes responsibility for completing the tasks. Nothing is communicated, nothing changes, nothing happens. This either adds to the "Why did we even have that meeting?" mentality or leaves you wondering, "Now what?"

The quality of the conversation does not directly correlate to the impact it will have. When there is ambiguity about next steps or who should take them, nothing gets done. If an item requiring action was not clearly stated as a task and given an owner, no one is going to do it. If it's seen as something that's optional, no one is going to do it. Period.

Even when the next steps are crystal clear, they mean nothing without accountability. If no one is keeping track of assignments that come from meetings or the team does not have a practice of looking at old notes before the next meeting, it's unlikely anything will get done at all. Those tasks remain forever in the notes, again begging the question of why you even had the meeting in the first place.

CHAPTER ONE REVIEW

- Bad meetings lack a clear purpose.
- Bad meetings are a distraction from your "real work."
- Having a day packed with back-to-back meetings is generally not a good thing.
- Don't use meetings as a solution for every single problem.
- People should be allowed to say "no" to meetings.
- Bad meetings happen when people don't prepare.
- Bad meetings bring out the worst in people.
- Lack of follow-through can turn even the best meeting into a wasted one.

CHAPTER ONE ACTION CHECKLIST

- Reflect on your own experiences with poor meetings:
  - Which of the pain points resonate most for you?
  - Which of the pain points have you observed in your organization?
  - Do you have other meeting pain points that weren't mentioned?
- Ask a colleague about his or her experience with meetings and listen wholeheartedly. Be open to sharing your experience if he or she is willing to listen.
  - How do these pains affect you, your team, and/or your whole organization?
  - What is the impact of poorly run meetings?
  - Do you think it's possible to change?

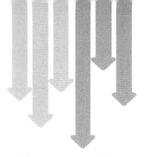

Chapter Two

Poor Meeting Practices Are Sabotaging Your Success

Companies have plenty to lose when the issues contributing to bad meetings are not addressed. According to a popular study by Verizon Conferencing, US companies waste at least $37 billion a year in unproductive meetings. But the losses don't stop there. Poor meetings can harm your organization's culture. They impact the quality of the work experience, souring the environment and increasing employee dissatisfaction. Ultimately, this can result in increased employee turnover and negatively impact your organization's bottom line. Even when employees stay, their work product can suffer if they're overly stressed, feel underappreciated, or have frustrating relationships with their colleagues. All these pains are linked to unproductive meetings.

MONEY MATTERS

It's easy to calculate how much money is spent per person to attend a meeting, but companies that pay their employees salaries rarely consider the hourly cost. If you have 5 people in a meeting who are each paid $100 an hour, that meeting costs $500 for one hour. If each of those people is wasting a third of their time in that meeting, that's 167 wasted dollars. On average, people waste about four hours a week in meetings. So, when considering these 5 workers, that's a weekly loss of $672 a week, or $2,688 a month. Those numbers skyrocket once the salaries of senior managers making upwards of $200 an hour are factored in. The old cliché is true: Time is money.

Michael Mankins, Chris Brahm, and Gregory Caimi at Bain & Company, a prestigious strategy consulting firm, used data-mining tools to analyze how organizations schedule meetings and found how a weekly executive meeting causes ripple effects throughout an organization. They found that to conduct a weekly status meeting for the executives, business unit leaders need to hold 11 meetings just to prepare. These meetings require another 21 team meetings to synthesize the information or prepare for upper-level approval. To achieve that, another 130 preparation meetings are held to support the team meetings. So, in the end, one weekly executive meeting can cost a staggering 300,000 person-hours per year in an organization. That's 15 percent of an organization's collective time, just in meetings, which does not include time spent preparing for those meetings.

The bigger or more hierarchical your organization is, the more significant these numbers are. Compounded with the cost per hour number we estimated earlier, you cannot underestimate the amount of financial resources and hidden costs your organization spends on meetings.

If all the time and resources we spent in meetings led to comparable outcomes, none of this would matter. However, as previously established, numerous industry and academic studies show people feel over one-third of the meetings they attend are not necessary. Some research even indicates people think more than 60 percent of their meetings are unproductive and inefficient. Whether it's 33 percent or 60 percent, organizations are taking a major financial loss due to poor meetings.

The cost of solving some of these problems pales in comparison. Investing in meeting effectiveness workshops, webinars, book clubs, or even change initiatives costs relatively little in terms of time and money. Even using a software that facilitates effective meeting practices costs only a few dollars a month per person. I frequently tell Meeteor clients that for ten dollars per person per month, they can eliminate at least one unproductive meeting, and they will have already recouped their investment.

What if organizations managed time with the same intensity they gave to managing money? Consider the attention spent on budgeting. No one would tolerate knowingly wasting 5–10 percent of the budget, so why do we allow that to happen with our time?

HARMING CULTURE

Bob Pothier, Director of Partners in Leadership and a former GE executive said, "The strongest message about how you want your culture to perform is embedded in how you conduct your meetings." There is an explicit connection between how you want your organization to perform and how you conduct your meetings.

What your organization values is expressed through its culture and therefore influences how meetings happen.

What is culture? Culture is the set of beliefs and behaviors that direct people in how they act and interact. Simply put, it's often considered "the way we do things around here." Culture impacts how people feel—whether respected or undervalued—and the atmosphere of the work environment—collegial or competitive. It's your culture that celebrates go-getters or finger-pointers. Whatever the culture has deemed appropriate behavior is how people will act and interact.

Sometimes your organizational culture proclaims to be one thing, but your meetings don't reflect that. The reality is, what your culture values is going to show up in your meetings, for better or for worse. If you want a results-oriented culture and yet your meetings are not achieving their goal, that's a problem. You need your meetings to be results-oriented as well in order to perpetuate a culture of accomplishment. Alternatively, if you want innovation to be a part of your core culture, you need your meeting practices to align with a culture of innovation. In this case, meetings should foster open and exploratory conversation, emphasize learnings from customers over personal opinions, and keep good records of ideas and decisions. Soul-crushing meetings don't help create an environment ripe for innovation.

People look for cues in their environment to help them understand what behaviors are expected. At an international manufacturing company we've worked with, debating and pushing back on leadership is not only acceptable but celebrated. This company has created a culture in which all voices and perspectives are welcome. This comes to life when making decisions in meetings. Everyone can argue with the boss to develop and enhance an idea. The senior person in the room might ultimately make the final decision, but this doesn't mean they have all the answers. To get to the best outcome, it's expected that dissenting voices will speak up, people will play devil's advocate, and alternative ideas will be put on the table.

This is all done in a way that is very respectful and helpful, yet this behavior is not typical at most companies. Usually people are deferential to their bosses, backing off when senior people state their opinions, even if their ideas are not the best ones.

Imagine you are a new mid-level employee. You sit in your first meeting with senior leaders and see a mid-level manager argue with the CEO. *That person must be crazy! Is he trying to get fired?* you might think. Then, of course, that manager is not fired and this culture of open debate happens again and again. Over time, you begin to understand the culture at this new company is not the same as your prior organization. You too will become comfortable with the idea that you should argue with the boss, present alternatives, and question decisions. This is one example of how someone uses cues to figure out how to act in a new environment.

Culture is expressed in many ways and comes up frequently in activities associated with meetings. A few of the more common expressions of culture are routines, rituals, language, habits, symbols, and norms. Each provides a specific mode that reinforces the values and messages about the organization or team's culture. These elements can be positive when they support healthy, productive actions, and feelings. They become negative when they foster frustration or unproductive behavior.

ROUTINES

Routines, according to the *Oxford American College Dictionary*, are "a sequence of actions regularly followed." Routines simplify actions done on a regular basis by providing a standard, accepted approach.

Thoughtful, shared routines within a company or organization simplify a process. If a behavior is established as a routine, it doesn't matter who takes the action, it will be the same. This increases the likelihood of success and reduces the mental energy needed to accomplish the activity.

One common routine is the creation of an agenda. When there is a shared routine for agenda creation, it doesn't matter who creates the meeting agenda. It will always include the same elements and be shared at least 24 hours in advance, assuming that's what the culture has deemed acceptable. If, for some reason, the meeting leader deviates from this routine, the team will recognize it and respond accordingly. In one business I know of, if an agenda is not sent at least 24 hours in advance, the meeting is automatically canceled. No ifs, ands, or buts.

Similarly, a team might have a routine regarding meeting notes. What happens to notes after the meeting might vary from person to person; but, when there is a shared routine, the team can rely on the fact that no matter who took the notes, they will be typed and emailed within 24 hours of the meeting's conclusion, and a digital copy will be stored in the appropriate file. Routines create consistency and reduce the cognitive load, or brain power, required to perform the actions.

RITUALS

Rituals, unlike routines, are the practices that elevate the meeting experience by making them special. They are designed to enhance the moment via relationship building, learning, celebration, or otherwise. Teams can have rituals regarding how meetings start, such as using a check-in to ask, "How is everyone doing today? What's on your mind?" This particular ritual helps build relationships and collegiality among meeting attendees, preparing them for the conversation at hand.

Kim Scott, author of *Radical Candor: Be a Kick-Ass Boss without Losing Your Humanity*, shared one interesting ritual to shape a positive team culture: bring a stuffed monkey to team meetings. She called it "Whoops the Monkey." In the meeting, she asked people to share a mistake they've made in the previous week. Whoever shares a story gets forgiveness immediately. Then, team members applaud for the best failure story, and that person wins Whoops for the week. This ritual encourages team members to reflect on their mistakes and helps them feel more comfortable being vulnerable in front of colleagues. It's a powerful way to facilitate a culture of learning and feedback.

Rituals can energize people and create delightful and magical moments that are unique to your team.

LANGUAGE

Shared language is a fundamental component of any culture. If you've ever been new to an organization that has its own terminology, you've likely experienced that terrifying moment of feeling confused and out of the loop. Different companies define terms in different ways. What some call a "goal" and "metrics," others call an "objective" and "measures." Using the wrong terms is embarrassing, as is not understanding what's being said. As soon as you know an organization's specific words or phrases, you're instantly in the club.

Meetings are filled with cultural language that can seem like organizational jargon. One company might say, "Let's put that idea in the parking lot," whereas another could reference the holding bin that houses off-topic ideas as a "back burner." When you hear someone say, "Take me from the 40,000-foot view to the 5,000-foot view," you might be able to intuit what she means, but it's not totally obvious. Is there also a 100,000-foot view? What about a 100-foot view?

It doesn't mean the more jargon you use, the better your culture will be. It's about using shared language to stay aligned and encourage agreed-upon behaviors. The language a team uses both fosters the types of conversations and experiences of the team and creates an unspoken bond among members. The shorthand makes it easier and faster to elicit the behavior and desired experience in the meeting.

HABITS

There are both good habits and bad habits. In the case of meetings, helpful habits include actions such as using video conferencing instead of phone calls whenever possible. There isn't a rule that requires video—it's just something people do. On the other end of the spectrum, you can have bad habits such as a team leader always arriving 5 minutes late for every meeting. This wasn't a decision made by the team or an explicit action stated by the team leader. It's just a habit he's developed over the course of time.

Habits speak to the culture as well. When a leader sits at the head of the table, it says something about how she feels about her authority in the room. In Meeteor company meetings, which include colleagues participating virtually, Mamie sometimes sits at the head. It's the most direct seat for the camera, and Mamie is often facilitating these meetings, so it's important for her to be clearly seen. But she doesn't always sit there. Instead, colleagues are encouraged to rotate seats so everyone takes turns sitting in the "position of power."

It takes concerted effort to change a habit or develop a positive one to begin with. Bringing attention to the things people do subconsciously can help them realize how their habits are contributing to a positive or negative meeting culture.

SYMBOLS

Have you ever been in a meeting with a talking stick or facilitator hat? How about little green flags? I've been in meetings with all three, although not at the same time. These items are symbols imbued with meaning by the group. If you are new to the team, you might be confused by the items because you don't understand the specific and special meaning they have for this culture.

That's how I felt the first time I was in a meeting with those little green flags. Participants would pick up the flags in front of them seemingly at random, and sometimes put them back down. Finally, when I was the last person without a flag, the meeting leader called me out. "Mamie, what's keeping you from agreeing with this decision? I haven't heard you say anything contrary yet." I was bewildered. I agreed with the decision and wasn't sure why the meeting leader thought I didn't. He then explained that their practice is to pick up the flag once you're on board with the idea, and then put it back down if that changes. In this way, as soon as all the flags are picked up, it means the group has reached consensus.

Despite feeling a bit embarrassed for being called out and frustrated no one had explained this ritual, I was also highly impressed with this team. The green flags symbolized your feelings about the decision. They'd made something invisible—your feelings—visible by giving them a physical symbol, thus enabling their decision-making process to move more quickly.

NORMS

Norms are the ground rules that guide people's behavior. They are shared practices, both written and unwritten, everyone is expected to follow. In a meeting, you might see a norm of arguing with the boss, or playing devil's advocate. Norms, like other culture elements, can be both positive and negative. Many teams have a norm of showing up late to meetings without consequence. Everyone knows that meetings don't start on time, so it's acceptable to arrive a few minutes after the given start time.

There are all kinds of norms that influence culture and meetings. Some teams write norms on a board or include them in the agenda. When meeting norms are explicit, it empowers the group to hold each other accountable to specific behaviors, such as speaking from a place of "yes, and" or making room for quieter voices. When the norms are not clearly defined or explicitly shared with a group, it can take people additional energy and time to figure out or negotiate what behaviors are expected in the moment. Read more about norms in Chapter Nine.

KILLING PRODUCTIVITY

Meetings are one of the largest time wasters in organizational life today, along with excess emails and constant interruption. As previously mentioned, employees attend a ridiculous number of meetings, a whopping one-third of which are considered a waste of time. This is not only terrible for all of us sitting in those horrible meetings, but it's crushing our productivity.

Productivity is "the measure of efficiency in converting inputs into useful outputs." In other words, it's a measure of how much we are accomplishing, given our resources. How well are we using our time and energy? It's about the quantity and quality of your work, and it can be impacted by many factors.

LOST TIME

The most obvious link between productivity and meetings is the time lost by participating in a meeting that either didn't move the work forward or that you didn't need to be in. In both cases, the opportunity cost of your participation is equivalent to everything else you could have done during that hour.

Time is a precious, non-renewable resource, so if you're wasting it in a meeting, you can't spend it on other more important things. In some cases, this is what drives us to work after hours. To make up for the time lost in meetings, we stay late and miss dinner with the family, open our laptops while lying in bed, or skip that 6:00 a.m. run to get to the office early. These are all attempts to maintain the outputs expected of us and allow us to engage in deeper, more focused work. Yet while work is technically getting things done and deadlines aren't being missed, organizations are risking employee's well-being and compromising the quality of work. A study conducted by Harvard Medical School shows sleep deprivation is costing $63.2 billion in lost productivity for US businesses. Imagine if you could take two or four or even eight extra hours back from meetings each week to get things done during the workday. That would increase productivity, while also enabling you to have a healthy life outside the office.

Professor Leslie Perlow and collaborators at Harvard Business School surveyed 182 senior managers in a wide range of industries on how meetings impact their work. Sixty-four percent of respondents said, "Meetings come at the expense of deep thinking." When leaders' calendars are run by their meetings, it leaves little time for them to do deep-thinking work. This not only harms productivity; it hinders innovation and strategic thinking.

UNNECESSARY CONFUSION

Successful meetings produce next steps, but how these action items and decisions are captured and managed can either boost productivity or detract from it. I've observed people record meeting notes on sticky notes, in notebooks, or in email or other digital documents. Most of the time, these are not the final meeting notes that get shared with all participants and other key stakeholders, nor are they the person's primary task or knowledge management system.

When it comes to sharing information after a meeting, someone needs to type up the decisions and next steps and communicate them. If this doesn't happen, all those in attendance have their own records of the meeting, which may have different versions of what was agreed to. If you didn't attend the meeting, you might hear different outcomes depending on who you spoke to, adding to the confusion of what really happened.

Individual notes may not be easily searched, making it hard to find the information, such as a previous decision, when you need it. If you don't store notes in a consistent manner, you might waste time looking in your email, a folder, or your notebook, trying to find that particular meeting's record. Lack of shared notes communicated to all key stakeholders and easily accessed in the future generally leads to misalignment and the need to revisit old conversations.

UNCLEAR OUTCOMES, UNNECESSARY WORK

One challenge with ambiguous meeting outcomes is the uncertainty of what to do next. When you walk out of a meeting and you're not sure what to do, or you think you know what to do but you're not sure if everybody agrees, you either don't do anything, or worse, you do the wrong thing. Doing unnecessary work is a productivity and morale killer.

"Jane" called me in a panic one Friday afternoon asking if I could look over a document she urgently needed to get to our boss, "Marco." I asked her what the rush was about, given that Marco likely wasn't going to look at the document until Monday. Jane replied, "Marco said he wanted this document at our meeting yesterday, and I don't want him to think I'm ignoring his request." I was in that meeting, and Marco did not ask for that document directly. He asked if it existed and suggested we might want to pull the information together. He didn't assign it to Jane or give her a deadline of 5:00 p.m. Friday. I'm sure Marco would have been happy that we took his advice, but Jane was adding work to her plate, and now mine, without a good reason. After calming her down, I agreed to look at it on Monday morning for a few minutes. I also suggested she ping Marco to find out if he even wanted to see it and, if so, by when. I had an inkling he didn't actually want to review the document and was more concerned that we as a team were thinking about and paying attention to the right information.

Unfortunately, scenarios like this happen all too frequently. No one wants to be caught off guard for not having done work assigned to them. At the same time, it's really frustrating to be told, "Oh, that's not what we decided on. All that work you just did isn't useful."

CRUSHED MORALE

Remember that feeling you had sitting in your last unproductive meeting? I'd venture to guess you walked out with low energy, feeling drained, and in a bad mood. You got back to your desk and had trouble focusing. Despite having lots to do, you weren't about to produce your finest work. Crappy meetings leave everybody feeling down.

Doing extra work, doing the wrong work, feeling like you're in a meeting you don't need to be attending, feeling disrespected by your colleagues who talk over you or shut down your ideas—these impact your morale and the workplace atmosphere. A sour environment is not one in which people are eager to share ideas, collaborate, communicate, and produce their most efficient and high-quality work.

Your boss is also a critical factor in both your morale and your productivity. A 2015 Gallup study, "State of the American Manager," concluded that "managers account for 70 percent of the variance in employee engagement scores." A boss who drags you to unproductive meetings is wasting your time. If she doesn't encourage your participation or value your input, you might feel demotivated. If she doesn't help crystalize next steps or assign clear responsibilities to you, you might feel lost and confused when the meeting ends. Those feelings actually drain your energy. It's hard to be inspired to do your best work when you don't feel good about your colleagues, boss, or work environment.

ADDED STRESS

All these challenges produce stress, which itself negatively impacts productivity, creating an unhealthy negative spiral. Stress and frustration rise when you waste time in meetings and watch your to-do list pile higher with each passing moment. A 2014 study by Tower Watson shows when you're stressed, you're not working your best. Employees reporting high levels of stress take almost double the sick days as their less-stressed counterparts. Sustained, chronic stress—the kind we face daily at work—increases levels of cortisol in the brain, according to the *Be Brain Fit* article, "12 Effects of Chronic Stress on Your Brain." The higher the level of cortisol, a hormone that regulates metabolism and the immune response, the higher the chances of a variety of productivity-related problems: forgetfulness and learning challenges, emotional sensitivity, reduced cognitive function, increased risk of mental disease, and depression.

When you let bad meetings occur over and over, you kill morale, ruin people's health, waste time, create ambiguity and sometimes unnecessary work, and damage the relationship between yourself and your colleagues or employees.

CHAPTER TWO REVIEW

- Bad meetings cost money—more than any company or organization can afford.
- Organizations carefully manage money, but give little thought to managing time.
- Culture is a reflection of what an organization values. It guides how people act and interact and is expressed as routines, rituals, language, habits, symbols, and norms.
- Good meetings employ components of culture in a positive way to strengthen relationships and help everyone be at their best.
- Bad meetings damage culture and contribute to a negative work environment.
- Bad meetings crush productivity by wasting time, killing morale, creating unnecessary work, and adding stress.

CHAPTER TWO ACTION CHECKLIST

- Reflect alone or with your colleagues on how poor meetings are impacting your work.
- Calculate the cost of your meetings by visiting this website: hbr.org/2016/01/estimate-the-cost-of-a-meeting-with-this-calculator
- How does your culture support or inhibit effective meetings? Consider each element of culture individually and the culture as a whole.
- Document the answers from the three questions above and

refer to it later in Chapter Fourteen to build a business case for changing your meeting culture.

- What are some ways to create an awareness of the meeting problems with your team or organizational leadership? Write down two to three ideas to get the attention of your team, or jump to Chapter Fourteen for more inspiration.

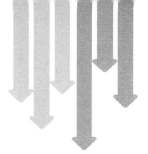

Chapter Three

Why Do These Problems Exist?

Meetings are not new to the workplace. Even with the increase in dispersed teams, conference calls, and virtual meetings, the challenges with meetings haven't changed much. We might have different technical difficulties to manage, but the heart of what makes an effective meeting is the same, regardless of where or how the meeting occurs. So, why are we still struggling with consistently holding productive meetings?

THE STIGMA OF NOT KNOWING

While most people agree there is a problem, few want to own the fact that they are contributing to it. It's not your meetings that are so terrible, but your boss's meetings or the guy from Marketing who's running the project. There is almost a stigma associated with admitting you need help to have good meetings. It might seem embarrassing to tell your colleagues, "I'm going to a workshop that's all about how to take notes," or, "I'm taking a course on effective meeting management." They are such common activities, they often feel administrative rather than strategic. We collectively undervalue the importance of being a skilled meeting leader or note-taker. Thus, we overlook or avoid the need to develop these competencies.

LACK OF TRAINING

Few people have experienced any form of education on effective meetings, and this lack of training contributes to the epidemic of bad meetings in many organizations. For the most part, we assume managing meetings is easy or anyone can figure it out, yet clearly this is not the case. Yes, some people are naturally inclined toward process and structure, and these folks will plan and run meetings effectively without much external influence. The rest of us will learn from experience. If we're lucky, we'll have a boss or colleague who excels at running meetings and who role models or shares their practices with us; although, even that offers no guarantee we'll understand or adopt his or her approaches. Ideally, we'd learn the art and science of effective meetings as young professionals, but the subject is largely absent from any corporate training or personal and professional development resources.

Unfortunately, there are not many options for getting help. If you want to learn how to code, or develop leadership skills, or pursue any other knowledge within your industry, there are likely an abundance of books, workshops, and courses to help you. Resources on meetings, however, are limited.

IT'S HARD TO MEASURE ROI

The impact of productive meetings on an organization's people and performance is hard to measure. There are few hard metrics that can be linked between certain types of cause and effect. A strong, healthy organizational culture has been linked with high employee engagement and low employee turnover, but there is yet to be empirical data directly tying these to effective meetings. Recent studies have identified some correlations between meetings and overall performance. For example, Simone Kauffeld of Technische Universität Braunschweig, and Nale Lehmann-Willenbrock of the University of Amsterdam, found some dysfunctional meeting behaviors, such as going off topic and criticizing ideas, were associated with lower levels of market share, innovation, and employment stability. Another study by Professor Steven Rogelberg, and colleagues, at the University of North Carolina shows a correlation between workers who perceive low meeting effectiveness with low job satisfaction. Yet, there are so many different factors that impact performance, which can differ from one organization to another. Additional research is surely needed but, even without it, we can all feel the difference between a culture of healthy and unhealthy meeting practices.

In addition, the financial returns are hidden. To change the practices, people must invest time and money in training or adopting new software. This feels like an outlay of resources, whereas the savings are buried. A company must pay a person's salary regardless, so the hundreds of dollars "saved" by attending fewer unproductive meetings is not a true savings, but rather a redeployment of resources while that individual attends to other work. It's almost impossible to measure the time saved by not having a bad meeting. Making the link from forward investing to greater organizational results is not an obvious direct line.

SENIOR LEADERSHIP ISN'T OWNING THE PROBLEM

Senior leaders are focused on improving the bottom line, making customers happy, or growing their market share. An increasing number have started thinking about employee engagement and retention. Some have even started gathering data around organizational culture. Yet few leaders have realized that meetings play a role in achieving all these goals, and even fewer are taking action to own the problem and address it with the seriousness other business areas receive. Individual team leaders might try to address the problem on their own; however, without leadership support and attention from the top, companies end up with sporadic practices.

NO STANDARD FOR MEETINGS

Another common cause of unproductive meetings is a lack of shared processes and tools within companies. Many companies lack standards for planning and facilitating meetings, as well as for following through on meeting action items. If every time you sit down to plan an agenda you must think about the kind of information you need—exact outcome, agenda items, norms, etc.—in addition to what the answers are, you are making the task more arduous than needed. Plus, it's likely that, on occasion, you'll forget to include some key components of your typical agenda.

The same is true for meeting participants. Imagine if every time you received a meeting agenda, it was in a different format and used different terminology. Some leaders refer to the desired outcome as the "meeting goal," others say "objective," still others say "purpose." Some people include agenda information in the calendar invitation, some send it in an email or as an attachment, and some only include logistical information without a clear plan. It takes more mental energy to process the information when we're attending to the content and the format. Using the same template each time allows the meeting planner and participant to focus on content rather than structure so everyone can quickly grasp the information.

Simply having a template does not guarantee a shared standard among different teams or individuals. You also need consistent application of the templates via a shared process or protocol. I've seen this at many organizations. As the staff count grows or long-time employees move on and are replaced by new people, what was once a standard practice becomes a thing only the old-timers do. When new employees are handed a template but not educated on the tool and trained on its use, a culture that initially had consistent usage can slowly dissipate as people misuse the tool or opt for their own approach.

At the end of the day, routines and structure make life easier for all of us. Once you've done something enough times, you no longer have to think about it as much. It's one of the reasons Steve Jobs and Mark Zuckerberg wore the same thing every day: It was one less decision they had to make. When you're not sure whether you should send the meeting materials in advance by email or whether you should be taking notes from one meeting to the next, you're unnecessarily taxing your brain. These uncertainties add to your mental load and can impact not only your meetings, but also your overall performance.

MEETINGS ARE A CYCLE, NOT AN EVENT

Unproductive meetings don't happen in the moment. They originate from a lack of clear understanding among the group of what needs to take place before, during, and after. A meeting is not only what happens once you're all gathered in the same room. Each meeting goes through a complete cycle, beginning with preparation, moving to execution of the agenda, and ending with follow-through. Without proper attention paid to each element, the structure fails.

The experience of a meeting often goes something like this:

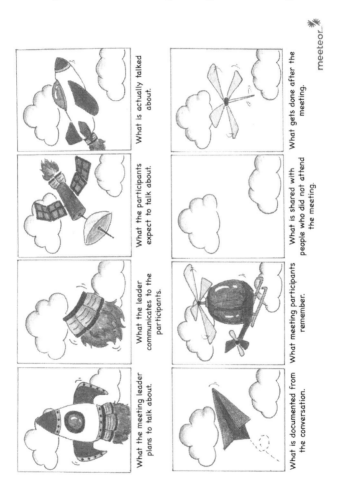

- The meeting leader has grand plans for what she wants to accomplish, but she keeps it mostly in her head.
- She shares a bit of information in the calendar event or by email, such as the title of the meeting or a sentence about what the group will do during the meeting.
- Participants, having such little information, fill in the blanks and imagine the meeting to have some other focus.
- In the meeting, the conversation wanders, and what is actually talked about isn't what anyone was prepared for.
- There is very little documented during the meeting. Maybe a few people scratched some notes for themselves, but there is no collective set of agreed-upon notes.
- A few days or weeks later, people debate what decision was made or can't remember who said they were going to do what.
- People who weren't in the meeting were told nothing, creating more confusion about what's going on.
- Finally, a follow-up task or two gets done, but no one is keeping track and it's unclear whether that task was even necessary.

When it comes to meetings, the opportunities for confusion, frustration, and derailment are many. Therefore, it's helpful to think about the various phases of a meeting in order to attend to them all with the attention they need.

DELAYED GRATIFICATION ISN'T SATISFYING

Another part of the problem stems simply from how our human brains work. No one enjoys delayed gratification, a phenomenon widely discussed after the famous Marshmallow Experiment at Stanford University in the 1970s. It takes self-control to intentionally give up immediate rewards to attain the benefits for a longer-term goal. People know a thoughtful agenda means a higher likelihood of an effective meeting, but planning an agenda offers little satisfaction in the moment. In fact, it's often the opposite, where you feel more stressed because you have to plan the agenda instead of attending to other work.

The act of writing and sending the agenda doesn't come with much extrinsic reward. Maybe you'll receive feedback or a "thank you" from your colleagues but, in most cases, you must wait until the meeting to get the real reward. In the meeting, you might notice the conversation is productive and you've achieved good outcomes, but your brain will not necessarily attribute the positive outcomes to the thoughtful agenda planning you did in advance.

One common misconception is that planning a meeting takes too much time. Someone once emailed me after using Meeteor software for the first time. He wrote, "I planned four meetings and it took me 45 minutes. That's so much time!" My response was the opposite. "You planned four meetings in 45 minutes— that's awesome!" I wrote. "You spent a little over 10 minutes on each agenda. That is not a lot of time to set your team up for a productive hour together." The next time I heard from him, he reported those meetings went well, and he saved at least that much time in the long run by not having to plan any follow-up meetings. Planning does take time, but not nearly as much as you might think. Sometimes we are held back by our own mental barriers. The truth is, by the time you are writing an agenda, you have already done the bulk of the thinking. You already have ideas brewing in your head on why you want to meet. Now you just need to put it on paper.

CALENDAR TOOLS AREN'T THE SAME AS MEETING TOOLS

Managing your calendar and managing a meeting are two completely different things, yet many meetings get planned solely through calendar invitations. The meeting name and a line or two in the description box aren't nearly enough to serve as a thoughtful meeting agenda. People look to that calendar event as the source of information for everything they need to know about the meeting. Google Calendar and Microsoft Outlook have over-simplified meetings as only a form of scheduling. They don't give participants everything they need for a successful meeting.

MEETINGS SEEM LIKE AN EASY ANSWER

There is a misconception that meetings can be easy and fast. Just ask your executive assistant to find a time, or send a doodle, or walk over to someone's desk. As the meeting leader, you may prepare a presentation, but other than that, you're good to go. As a participant, you don't need to prepare much at all—just show up. People view meetings as less work than writing a memo that explains the situation and gathering feedback, with endless follow-up reminders asking for responses. They think, "All I have to do is schedule the time and then sit in there and talk." This is far from the truth, as scheduling a meeting does not guarantee results.

WE DON'T BELIEVE IT CAN BE ANY OTHER WAY

Unfortunately, I've spoken to too many people who see bad meetings as a fact of life, a "necessary evil." They've become jaded to the idea that meetings can be consistently productive with a reasonable amount of effort. Maybe they've tried to change and found it too hard. Maybe the problem feels too big, like solving global hunger, and they can't even begin to imagine how to tackle the problem. Or maybe, the evil you know is better than the evil you don't. Bad meetings might appear be a lower risk than enacting changes, because people are already familiar with them and have put up with unproductive meetings for such a long time. Or maybe it's some entirely other reason.

DESPITE ALL THE PROBLEMS, CHANGE IS POSSIBLE

To have a fully functioning meeting culture—people, process, and tools—you must have clearly defined meeting processes and consistently apply them throughout your organization. For that to happen, staff must be confident in meeting best practices and facilitation, including those specific to your organization. Lastly, appropriate tools that can be used before, during, and after meetings should be available and applied. This isn't as easy as snapping your fingers, but it's no more challenging than many other culture change programs.

Organizations have survived greater internal changes. The key is to recognize that change takes time and effort. You must be willing to let go of your old ways and embrace the new. This means reshaping mindsets and behavior, which presents challenges, but is not impossible. Resources are available, starting with this book.

CHAPTER THREE REVIEW

- Meetings are not new, and neither are bad meetings. There are many reasons why the problems leading to bad meetings are so pervasive.
- There is a real lack of training around holding effective meetings. People are not taught how to manage meetings. Everyone assumes everyone knows how, when in fact, few do.
- No one wants to admit they don't know how to run a good meeting.
- The impact of improved meetings is hard to measure, but everyone knows when things are bad.
- Planning a meeting often requires delayed gratification, which no one loves, but it's well worth it in the long run.
- Companies lack shared practices around meetings, leading to inconsistency and confusion.
- Sending a calendar invitation is not the same as planning a meeting.
- While there are many problems surrounding the culture of meetings, there's good news. None of these road blocks are insurmountable, and if you're reading this book, you're already ahead of the game.

CHAPTER THREE ACTION LIST

- Which of the reasons bad meetings exist resonate most for you, your team, and your organization? Make a note of these reasons and read on.

- Has your organization, leadership, or team recognized the need for better meetings? Provided training on effective meetings? Have standard meeting tools, templates, and processes? Offered support for enacting changes to your meetings? If yes, what has worked and what hasn't?
- What other reasons do you think your team or organization struggles to recognize or take action on the problem of bad meetings?

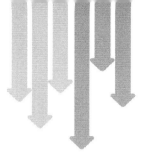

Chapter Four

So Why Have Meetings?

With all the challenges that meetings create, why not just stop having them all together? Because eliminating them would only raise a whole new set of challenges.

When meetings are done well, they are a boost to productivity. Meetings are capable of catapulting work forward by providing a space for team members to make decisions, build relationships, share and enhance ideas, solve problems, think creatively and critically together, learn from one another, and move into alignment. Meetings have the power to foster great, collaborative environments that cultivate trust and unity.

There is hope. Meetings, when done well, are an effective use of time and a great way to get work done together. Meetings should move work forward and build momentum, contributing to achieving the team's goals.

Meetings are not the problem. Bad meetings are the problem.

GET BETTER, FASTER RESULTS

Meetings help ignite thinking. A meeting creates the opportunity for synergy among the participants, resulting in deeper, more insightful thinking than would otherwise emerge. Interacting in person, whether physically together or not, provides a different level of understanding. You have a chance to ask follow-up questions and build on each other's ideas. The cyclical and organic nature of conversation allows people to contribute ideas and perspectives, and evolve their thinking as they process what the group is sharing. By responding to what others are saying, we are able to elevate our own thinking, connect ideas, and have new thoughts to share.

Other collaboration platforms don't allow for the richness of conversation that comes from a meeting. Shared documents tend to be linear in that people provide input one at a time, but don't typically go back to the document to reflect on what colleagues have shared after their initial contribution. Online chats tend to be unfocused, short, and less precise due to the fleeting nature of the chat stream.

When you bring a group of people with diverse perspectives together in the same "room," you increase the potential for richer outcomes. Research shows a team made up of people with diverse experiences and areas of knowledge is better at decision making, prediction, and planning. If you are working alone, you are limited by your own capabilities. If you never create opportunities for the team to gather, you're missing out on the chance to take advantage of the synergy that comes from diversity.

In addition to enriched thinking, a well-run meeting helps a group get more done in the time you spend together than you would working in sequence. When everyone is together, you can quickly gauge levels of agreement, identify points of dissent, generate buy-in, and reach alignment.

Sometimes, going person by person makes sense, but sometimes it's too time consuming or leads to confusion. When everyone needs to be aligned on the information or agree to a single next step, it can be faster and simpler to pull people together than to go one by one. You might have experienced an email chain where, after a few "Reply Alls," you think, "Oh my gosh, can we just have a meeting about this? I can't even follow the train of thought or decisions we're making anymore." This is when meetings shine.

MEETINGS BUILD STRONG RELATIONSHIPS

Meetings build relationships in ways other communication platforms can't. No number of gifs or emojis can make up for looking someone in the eye and hearing his or her voice. When you feel connected to your team and enjoy working with them, you feel safer asking for help, sharing unfinished ideas, and asking tough questions. This is not to say you should conduct meetings solely for relationship building, but they can facilitate the process.

For example, even the chitchat that happens at the beginning of the meeting can help sustain relationships. A study by Joseph Allen and other researchers at the University of Nebraska shows pre-meeting small talk helps build rapport among meeting participants and even creates room for participants to think about how they could interact with others more effectively during a meeting. You miss out on this informal connecting when you circulate a shared document or email.

When you take the first few minutes to check in and learn about what's new with your colleagues, you feel more connected with them. As human beings, we need direct interactions. We need real-life conversations where we use our voices and see each other's faces to fully connect with, understand, and appreciate one another.

Nothing can replace being physically together, but that doesn't mean all meetings must be done in this manner. Video conferencing tools continue to improve in quality and should be used whenever possible; but, on occasion, it's worth the time and money to bring people together across geographies.

At Meeteor, we have people in five different countries. We all gather together for one week every year, during which time we emphasize relationship building in addition to work deliverables. After everyone returns home, we find the afterglow of our week together gives us renewed positive energy toward the team and each person. At this point, we're not able to be together more frequently, but that's okay. Through video conferencing, we're able to maintain, and even build upon the relationships across oceans.

MEETINGS AS A WAY OF LEARNING

Meetings create opportunities for people to learn from each other and grow together. When you work collectively to solve a problem, you generate new ideas, bounce them off each other, and help connect the dots. Members of a team bring their unique viewpoints and experiences to the meeting. When we listen to each other, we're able to develop a better understanding of our colleagues and learn from the diverse perspectives in the team.

In these meetings, you uncover insights that are unlikely to surface if there's no real-time sense-making and interaction. When you're interacting with others, you learn about yourself as well. Throughout the meeting process, you're constantly honing your communication skills through active listening, asking questions, managing conflict, and synthesizing ideas. You're training your creative muscles, advancing critical thinking, and developing your leadership capabilities. Meetings are one way to learn by doing and experiencing.

In addition to personal growth, your team also benefits from effective meetings. In fact, some meetings are specifically designed to elicit learnings about the team. For example, an "after action review," also called "a retrospective," "plus/delta," or "debrief," is a type of meeting that takes place periodically, mostly after a project has ended or a phase of work is complete. These meetings are specifically held to help your team reflect on how you work together, what you've learned, and areas where you can improve. The knowledge and understanding that emerges from these meetings become learnings to inform future actions. Numerous studies have shown the power of after action review meetings. In a 2013 study, researchers Eddy, Tannenbaum, and Mathieu indicate this type of meeting not only accelerates learning from experience, but teams that run this meeting show more effective teamwork and outperform their counterparts in general. Team performance is enhanced when you make time to collectively learn.

We practice what we preach at Meeteor as well. Our product team runs "retrospective" meetings every week to reflect on what they learned that week and how they can improve the work the following week. It's helpful for team members to feel grounded, voice their ideas and concerns, and course-correct in a short period of time. We also run this meeting with our external collaborators. Many of them have shared that this is one of the most helpful ways for them to reflect on the process, make sense of the learnings, and document them for future reference.

MEETINGS REINFORCE ORGANIZATIONAL CULTURE

As mentioned in Chapter Two, poor meeting practices can harm your organization's culture. On the flip side, when you employ effective meeting practices, meetings can be one of the most powerful ways to shape and reinforce your organizational culture. Meetings are an activity that permeates almost every employee's daily work life. If you start to build a meeting environment that's engaging and enjoyable and makes every participant feel like they are heard and valued, you're reinforcing the culture you'd like to build in your organization.

Don't underestimate the ripple effect meetings can have on your organization. Meetings can be a powerful lever for change. With better meetings, you may see an increase in employee retention, a decrease in sick days, and changes to other aspects of your business. As meetings become healthier, your organization becomes healthier.

BAD MEETINGS CAN'T BE SOLVED WITH ARBITRARY RULES

Meetings are necessary and facilitate organizational growth. The problems are the poorly run ones. How do you eliminate those bad meetings? I've seen many companies try to address their poor meetings by introducing arbitrary meeting rules. Sadly, what they are actually doing is ruining the opportunity for effective collaboration from the outset. An arbitrary approach to anything is useless. It doesn't address root causes and, in some ways, forces you into making poor decisions. It's far more important to address the cause of a problem and try to change those behaviors than to put a Band-Aid over them.

Many successful business leaders have created fads around arbitrary meeting rules. Jeff Bezos is famous for the "two-pizza rule": Never have more people in a meeting than can be fed by two pizzas. Why? I've participated in meetings with hundreds of people where great thinking emerges and decisions are made. It takes intention to design a meeting of that size, but all meetings require intentionality if you want them to be successful.

Another popular rule is "only have 30-minute meetings," based on the assumption people can stay more focused in shorter spurts. It's also tied to the old belief of "you'll use as much time as you have"; so, less time must mean more efficiency. Such a limitation can result in a variety of problems. You can make a decision in 30 minutes, but is it the best decision? Sometimes you need to dive deeper and explore options. Forcing a decision simply because of a random rule doesn't make sense.

Other times, you might end the meeting without a clear conclusion, resulting in the need for additional meetings so the team can have a complete conversation. There is a cost for every meeting. Each requires scheduling time, preparation, and follow up. Two 30-minute meetings are twice as much work as one 60-minute meeting, even though you get the same amount of meeting time.

In fact, you actually get more time in a 60-minute meeting than in two 30-minute meetings, due to the start-up and wind down time. Meetings never start exactly on time. Assume every meeting has 5 minutes of "getting in the room" time, during which people are walking or calling in, materials are being pulled up on the screen, etc. Then you have a few minutes of orienting the group to what the meeting is about and what you want to accomplish. Then, at the end of the meeting, you have a few minutes of wrapping up and reviewing next steps. Regardless of the length of the meeting, you can safely assume 5-10 minutes of entry and exit costs per meeting. So, for two 30-minute meetings, you get 40-50 minutes of conversation time. A single 60-minute meeting allows 50-55 minutes of dialogue. This may seem minor, but it's not.

In addition to the logistical costs, there are also mental costs. Every time a new meeting starts, the participants need to orient their brains to the topic at hand. They need to remember what was shared at the last meeting and try to avoid repeating or rehashing old conversation. Shifting mental gears takes energy, and going from short meeting to short meeting can be quite taxing.

Another approach that has gained popularity is "No Meeting Wednesdays." This is a great strategy for creating long periods of time for focused, deep work. It's hard to protect large blocks of time to attend to work that requires uninterrupted attention. Even when you block your calendar for a few hours on Tuesday mornings, if that's the best time for an impromptu meeting, you're hard pressed to say no just because you want your focus time.

Another benefit of no-meeting days is the reduction of low value time. If you have a meeting from 9:00 to 10:00 and another meeting at 10:30, the half hour in between is typically wasted. You can check email, maybe go through your task list, and then it's time to go to the other meeting. This is not enough time to do meaningful work. But beware: By forcing all your meetings into four days instead of five, you might experience the unintended consequence of having more of these low value times now that you have more meetings in any given day.

Having a day dedicated to truly focused work solves a related but different problem than unproductive meetings. In some cases, it's a great productivity booster, but it doesn't eliminate the need for all meetings, nor does it improve your meetings. They are not going to get any better just because they're not on Wednesdays.

BEGINNING THE CHANGE PROCESS

Now the question is, how do you turn bad meetings into effective, engaging, and enjoyable ones? I'll guide you through these practices and strategies throughout the book. But first, I'd like to acknowledge the feelings you might have right now. Maybe you're gung-ho, or maybe you're a bit intimidated. Mostly, leaders share with us their mix of emotions at this point in the journey. They have great enthusiasm, but also real concerns as they prepare to embark on the meeting transformation process. "I'm excited to start implementing effective meeting practices, but changing behavior is hard and our team's or organization's habit of holding bad meetings feels insurmountable," they say. If this is how you feel, don't fret. As is the case with any bad habit, the first step toward kicking it's assessing whether you have a problem with meetings and admitting it. If the descriptions in previous chapters resonate with you, you're not alone. The good news is you're already one step ahead because you're reading this book.

Ideally, the next step is for the entire team or organization to acknowledge something is wrong with the way meetings are run and commit to making them better. Change can be more powerful and sustainable when you do it with others. Most people would agree meetings are a problem. They may have even shared their frustrations or complaints with you in the past, but done nothing about them. The missing ingredients were a combination of awareness of what to do differently and motivation to do it. It's time to bring the problem to the surface, champion the issue, and work together toward finding and implementing solutions.

Getting everyone on board can be easier said than done. It's important to recognize that, for some people, meetings provide a sense of power, authority, and importance. They might have longstanding habits and behaviors deeply connected to their concepts of their job, which includes going to meetings. I know of one company that changed its practices and cut time spent in meetings in half. One manager told me, "I don't know what to do, because all I do is go to meetings, and now that I don't have to, I have nothing else to do with my time." His self-identity and role were deeply connected to meetings and the part he played in them. They shaped how he thought about his job. In these cases, people are not being lazy or intentionally disruptive. There are psychological factors influencing their feelings and reactions.

That being said, people do change for many reasons. When they understand why change is important and how they will personally benefit from it, implementing new practices becomes easier. For some people, numbers and facts are the most convincing reasons to change. Others are better served by stories, case studies, and accounts of firsthand experiences. Either way, it's essential to have a vision for the future where effective meetings help the organization or team as a whole, and each person individually, to make the concept more tangible and compelling.

This enables people to see what's possible and begin to address how they can get there.

Remember, I said the next step was *ideally* to get others on board. If you're ready, I recommend you go to Chapter Fourteen and learn how to generate buy-in for tackling your meeting challenges. If you're not ready to take the lead, that's okay too. There's plenty you can do on your own. You may feel more confident to share the need for change and potential solutions after reading additional chapters. Take your time and do what feels best for you, your team, and your organization.

EFFECTIVE MEETINGS ARE EVERYONE'S RESPONSIBILITY

Whether we primarily act as meeting leaders or participants, we all have an obligation to make the meeting successful. Each of us can contribute to productive meetings. If you rely only on yourself as the meeting leader, you're likely to become overwhelmed. That's a lot of pressure on one person. As a participant, if you're not helping, you're shirking your own responsibility as part of the group.

In some circumstances, it's harder, or impossible, to implement or support a practice on your own. Just because you're the leader doesn't mean you can always make changes without the support of your colleagues. That's okay. You don't need to enact every practice right away. The key is to do what you can, regardless of your role.

We heard a story of change from one of our blog readers who liked our ideas on implementing norms, which are practices a group accepts as standards for behavior (more on norms in Chapter Nine). She liked the idea of using norms in her team meetings, so she sent the article to her boss and quickly heard back. He said, "I think this is the stupidest thing in the world, but if you want to introduce it at the meeting and look like a fool, go for it." Sadly, not all bosses are great managers who care about and want the best for their team. Regardless, she decided to try it and introduced the concept to the whole team at their next meeting. She printed the article and circulated the hard copies. She explained the concept and asked everyone to read the article prior to their next meeting. The following week, she asked the group if they were willing to try using norms, and everybody was on board. Her boss was unhappy because he thought everyone would be in line with his way of thinking. Despite his disapproval, he'd already implicitly agreed to the approach by allowing her to present the concept to the group in the first place. He reluctantly agreed to try using norms, and we've heard numerous stories from this reader of how norms have helped her team work through difficult meeting behaviors. This story demonstrates that even in the most unfriendly environments, anyone can introduce new ideas and improve their meetings.

In each chapter, I address how to use the practices regardless of whether you are the meeting leader or a participant. I believe you and everyone on your team have the capacity to enact change and support effective meeting practices. Soon, you'll be the one telling these transformational stories.

CHAPTER FOUR REVIEW

- Meetings are not the problem. Poor planning and execution are the problem. In many ways, meetings can help people connect, problem solve, engage, and enjoy their work.
- Good meetings save time in the long run because everyone is working on the same page together, rather than separately while trying to stay informed about what everyone else is doing.
- Good meetings build and strengthen relationships.
- Arbitrary rules—such as no-meeting days or limiting the number of participants—can do more harm than good. Focus instead on effective approaches centered on what you really wish to accomplish.
- Admitting you have a problem is the first step. Then, once you have everyone on board, you can move forward together toward real change.
- When considering implementing new practices, remember, some people place great value on meetings in terms of defining their roles within the organization. Respect these feelings and use them to help propel everyone toward a better future.
- Remember also that people respond better to certain approaches: Some need data and numbers to help them see problems. Some rely on personal stories. Determine which approach will best serve you and use it to help everyone see the benefits that change will bring to them personally and to the entire organization.
- Effective meetings are everyone's responsibility.
- There is no one way to introduce change in your team or organization. Do what feels best for your situation.

CHAPTER FOUR ACTION LIST

- Are you getting healthy discussion and rich thinking from group conversation? If not, what might be holding you back?

- How frequently do you find chat or email communications becoming overly simplified or complex, resulting in the need for a meeting?

- Are you using adequate video conferencing tools to support relationship building during virtual meetings?

- Do you/your team members have enough time to do focused, deep work on a regular basis?

- Does your team or organization use any arbitrary meeting rules? If yes, how are they helping or hurting your meetings, productivity, culture?

- Visit Chapter Fourteen to learn more about raising the issue and generating buy-in for tackling your meeting challenges.

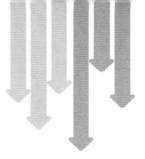

Chapter Five

Meetings Aren't for Everything

To give your meeting the best chance for success, there are a few questions you should ask before scheduling a date and time. These questions will help you determine whether you're truly in need of a meeting and whether a meeting is the appropriate form of collaboration to move you forward.

DO YOU REALLY NEED TO MEET?

As previously explained, it can seem easy to schedule a meeting to solve a problem, but a meeting can be costly in effort. When you understand what you need and the various options for how to engage your colleagues, you might find a meeting is wholly unnecessary. A fundamental component of creating an environment of effective meetings is using meetings to their full potential, and not holding meetings when an alternative would be better. When this happens, you should have fewer meetings overall, and those you do have will be much more productive.

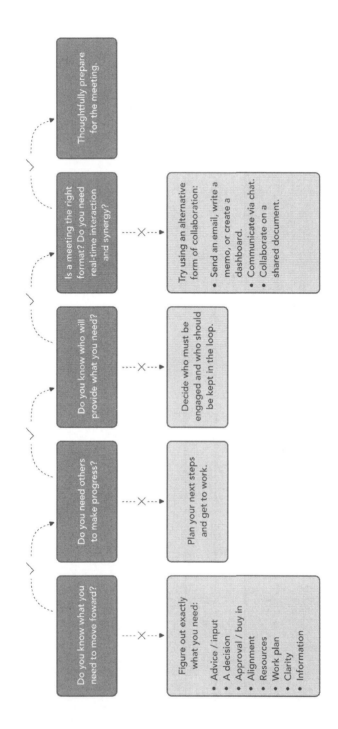

Thoughtfully prepare for the meeting.

Is a meeting the right format? Do you need real-time interaction and synergy?

Try using an alternative form of collaboration:

- Send an email, write a memo, or create a dashboard.
- Communicate via chat.
- Collaborate on a shared document.

Do you know who will provide what you need?

Decide who must be engaged and who should be kept in the loop.

Do you need others to make progress?

Plan your next steps and get to work.

Do you know what you need to move foward?

Figure out exactly what you need:

- Advice / input
- A decision
- Approval / buy in
- Alignment
- Resources
- Work plan
- Clarity
- Information

ARE YOU CLEAR ABOUT WHAT YOU NEED?

Have you ever had a moment when you find yourself staring at the computer screen feeling lost and unsure of what to do? I've had these moments, and my initial instinct is often to turn to a nearby coworker and ask for help. While it might ultimately help me move forward, it's often disruptive to whomever is being asked to stop what they're doing at that moment to tend to my needs. In essence, I'm asking for an emergency meeting. But is it really an emergency?

When you're stuck, it seems easier to grab another person than to rely on your own process or tools to move past the situation. This is particularly true for extroverts, who find it easier to think out loud when someone else is listening. Introverts are inside thinkers, so it's easier for them to think through situations on their own. It's the difference between talking to think and thinking to talk.

Instead of immediately turning to another person, start with a moment of reflection. Are you clear about the problem or decision you need to make? Do you know exactly what information, materials, or input is necessary to move the matter forward? If the answer to both is yes, you're still not ready for a meeting, formal or informal, but you can continue down the path of analysis. If the answer is no, you must figure out what the issue is and what you really need. This could be advice, information, a decision or approval, or to complete a task.

DO YOU NEED OTHERS' INPUT?

Once you know what you need, ask yourself if the input or work of others is required to help you get it. Sometimes you don't need anything from anyone else; if this is the case, do the work on your own. For example, one woman I spoke with shared a story about a time she needed help with Outlook. She thought about asking the "Outlook guru" in her office, but decided instead to do a search on YouTube first. Not surprisingly, she was able to quickly find a video that showed exactly what she needed to do.

If you do need others to make progress, think about who those people are. Try to differentiate between those who will provide what you need and those who should be kept in the loop. It's critical to have the right people participate. Otherwise, you're either unable to achieve the outcome you need or you've wasted the time of people who didn't contribute or receive value.

I once heard a story about a team that made it all the way to the end of the meeting before figuring out the person who was responsible for making the decision wasn't there. The discussion was quite rich and the group came to a sound conclusion, but they were unable to implement until the right senior leader signed off. Sadly, an email or memo would not suffice, given the gravity and complexity of the decision. Instead, another meeting with the same group of folks needed to be held to review the conversation this group just had in order to get buy-in from the senior leader. If only the meeting leader would have asked himself, "Who needs to be in the room in order to make this decision?" perhaps the original meeting invite would have included that necessary senior leader.

IS MEETING THE RIGHT FORMAT?

Once you know who is needed, decide whether the situation is complex, whether buy-in is important, or whether there is value in having real-time discussion. This is the moment to assess if a meeting is the right format. Meetings are ideal for issues with high complexity or when sense-making is needed. Meetings provide space for people to think collectively, listen to one another, and connect dots to shape reality. Not every situation requires this type of conversation.

When you're in need of feedback or advice, a meeting might not be the ideal setting. In meetings, people take turns speaking one at a time. If you have a 30-minute meeting of 5 people, assume the first 5 minutes are spent getting organized and the last 5 on a recap, which leaves 20 minutes for conversation. If there are 5 people in attendance, each one can talk for 4 minutes if there is balanced participation. In this case, you got 4 minutes of someone's thinking but took up 30 minutes of their time. Does that math make sense? In some cases, it might.

To help you determine whether a meeting is appropriate, consider whether one of the alternatives to a meeting will enable you to achieve the outcome you need, or at least serve as a starting point, which can lead to a meeting if needed (see more on meeting alternatives below). If you've concluded that a meeting is necessary, you are ready to invite others to join the meeting. Don't forget to share the desired outcome when you send the invite.

I urge you to go through this process each time you consider planning a meeting. Too often, people jump into planning meetings. After all, as renowned psychologist Abraham Maslow says, "I suppose it is tempting, if the only tool you have is a hammer, to treat everything as if it were a nail." In many organizations, a meeting might seem like an obvious solution. If you start by asking yourself what and who you really need, it could lead you in another direction.

MEETING ALTERNATIVES

There are several options that can produce similar results to having a meeting—each can help save you and your entire team both time and effort when used appropriately. No one option is better than another, but it's important to weigh the pros and cons of each and avoid overusing any one of them as the go-to form of collaboration.

EMAIL, MEMO, OR DASHBOARD

A meeting should rarely be held simply to inform participants or stakeholders. The exception to this practice is when the information is highly sensitive or complex, or stakeholder buy-in is needed. Most meetings primarily centered on information sharing should be replaced by an email or memo.

Instead of gathering the group together to speak about the information, draft an email or memo explaining whatever it is that you need to communicate. One organization I work with does this beautifully. The memos generally follow a structure that makes it very easy to grasp the information. They start by describing the situation or problem. Next, they describe solutions that were considered or are being proposed, followed by open questions or concerns. If a decision was already made, the memo concludes with the decision and who made it. If there is an action required, such as feedback or approval needed, the document ends with a clear call to action or description of next steps.

This format of situation + alternatives + watch-outs + results (decision/action) enables stakeholders to follow the thinking as if it were being presented live. The added benefit of using a memo instead of a presentation is that you are better able to control the message. It's easy to go off on a tangent, use the wrong words, or convey slightly different messages each time you repeat the presentation. A memo enables you to articulate the information effectively and consistently to all stakeholders at the same time.

Similarly, another alternative is to share information on a dashboard. This eliminates the need for reviewing data or statistics via presentation. If you find yourself sharing or receiving reports on the same information on a regular basis, this meeting might be a candidate for a dashboard. A solid dashboard can include numbers, charts, and graphs, but it can also include status updates on ongoing work.

The most important thing to consider when sending a memo, email, or dashboard is that you lose the guarantee each recipient will read it thoroughly. If you're concerned the material will not be read, I urge you to consider what should happen after the reader consumes the content. If the information you're sharing is urgent or important, you might want to follow up with each stakeholder to ensure they are informed. In this case, you might still spend 30 minutes meeting with people, but they each only need to spend 5 minutes with you.

ONLINE CHAT

Chat apps such as Slack, Yammer, Hipchat, and Microsoft Teams are helping cut down on meeting time. According to a 2015 study conducted by Slack, over 1,600 users reported an average of 24 percent reduction in number of meetings. Chat is ideal as an alternative to meeting when you have a quick question or want input on something that can be explained in approximately one paragraph. Chat is not designed for lengthy communications, and most have minimal options for text formatting, making it challenging to convey complex information.

However, chat does facilitate easy voting. For example, we have a book club at Meeteor. Each month, one staff member proposes a few options for what book the group should read next. Whomever is recommending books that month posts a message in Slack with the three titles and links to the books on Amazon or other sites where people can learn more. Everyone in the organization can then vote on which book they are most excited about reading. While this example is clearly not a critical business decision, it does demonstrate how easy it is to share options and request input. Just imagine how effective it can be when a quick vote is required related to something for which you'd otherwise have to meet.

 dan 🍴 12:40 PM
Speaking of which, here are my 3 nominations for the next book. Thoughts? or vote with a thinker, liar, or pair of jeans.

🙂 Thinking Fast and Slow
https://en.wikipedia.org/wiki/Thinking,_Fast_and_Slow

👤 Trust Me, I'm Lying
https://en.wikipedia.org/wiki/Trust_Me,_I%27m_Lying

🧬 The Gene: an intimate history
https://en.wikipedia.org/wiki/The_Gene:_An_Intimate_History
(edited)

🙂 4   👤 5   🧬 7

Chat is also ideal for replacing impromptu meetings meant to produce quick results. These informal meetings, where you grab a colleague and say, "Hey, do you have a minute?" are quite useful, but they can also be disruptive. Your coworker might be sitting at his desk focused on work, and you come in and interrupt his process and flow. An ideal solution to this less-than-desirable scenario is chat. By sending a chat message, you can communicate your needs, and the recipient can respond when it's convenient. Chat often elicits a faster response than email, and chat messages tend to be more concise. As long as your need can be addressed within a few hours without inhibiting you from being productive, ask your question or seek feedback by chat. You might be surprised that you can be more precise and concise in conveying what you need and your colleague can do the same in her response. When you sit down with someone, you might feel the need to over-explain things or say a lot that doesn't actually need to be said. When you chat, the simple act of typing your message almost forces you to be more precise because you only have space for a few sentences.

Another benefit to communicating via chat is the ability to make any conversation public. There are times when certain people need to be informed but don't need to take part in the conversation. When everyone can see the conversation and the outcome, they are able to stay informed without having to weigh in themselves. Most informal and impromptu meetings don't have notes written and circulated. This means not all stakeholders can be easily kept in the loop. If you opt, instead, to have a conversation by chat, it will be recorded and available to anyone who is part of that chat room. You can even tag specific people who need to be informed.

While chat can be a beneficial tool, it's important to take steps to create a healthy culture around chat. When it's not used appropriately, it can easily become a distraction. At Meeteor, we developed our own internal norms and practices for chat. We agreed to mention or tag specific people whose feedback or response was needed. That way, anyone who wasn't tagged knows their input is optional, and those who were necessary were alerted. We also agreed to include due dates for responses to avoid never-ending conversations.

We broke some of our larger topic rooms into smaller rooms to create more specificity for the conversations. For example, we initially had one chat room for all our technical development, but found people were getting lost in a mix of topics, issues, and questions they really didn't need to know about. We created smaller rooms that were more specific, such as dev-outlook-integration and dev-mobile-app, and wrote a purpose for each to prevent people from posting in the wrong places.

We also encouraged everyone to address their personal settings to indicate when they wanted to be disturbed and when they didn't, and which rooms they received notifications for. Turning off notifications to avoid the constant "ding" of a new message allows us to engage in deep, focused work without interruption.

Last, we acknowledged that when it comes to chat, people will get to things when they get to them. If something is critical or urgent, you should not rely on chat to communicate the message. This removes the pressure to be active on chat all day, constantly checking messages so you don't miss anything, or be immediately responsive to any incoming messages. Instead, chat is there when you are ready for it.

SHARED DOCUMENTS

Another alternative to meetings is shared documents or materials. There are occasions when you need input but not from everybody at the same time. When you are gathered in a meeting, only one participant can talk at a time, which is not always the best way to seek feedback or enrichment. Sometimes, creating a document or other material and asking people to respond directly within it is more efficient.

I learned this the hard way. A while ago, we had a meeting about Meeteor's mobile app design. The designer needed input from Mamie as CEO, Tai as our resident behavior change expert and customer success lead, our product manager, and our lead engineer. We sat together for an hour and barely made it past the first few slides. We had to take turns asking questions and sharing ideas. It was painfully slow, and we ended the meeting having more designs awaiting enrichment than we'd completed.

Soon after, we began using a software called InVisionApp to share designs and provide feedback. Now, the designer uploads the images, and we can all leave comments when it's most convenient for us within the deadline. The designer then reviews all the comments, and either uses her best judgment to make changes, brings an issue or vote to the group by chat, or calls a meeting to discuss a point of conflict. It saved us a lot of time, and the designs were iterated much faster.

There are many ways to create a shared document, whether you use Google Docs, InVisionApp, Dropbox, or any other online platform. What's important is that the author is able to create material and the platform allows people to leave feedback, comments, edits, and questions directly inside the document or image.

When you let people comment individually in a shared document, everyone can spend their own time thinking about the material, then respond thoughtfully to the material and each other. You might end up getting an hour of a person's devoted attention versus a quick ten minutes in a meeting.

As with chat, it's also important to have a system and norms for sharing such documents. Our practice at Meeteor is to use chat to post a link to that material, tag the people whose feedback is needed, and set a deadline for responding. We prefer this to sending the document by email, because it enables everyone in the chat room to be informed of the request, even if they are not required to give input. It's like cc'ing a bunch of people without cluttering their inboxes. Plus, chat is our primary form of internal communication. Whatever practice you have for informing people of a request for input on a shared document is fine, as long as there is clarity and consistency so everyone knows where to look.

Shared documents also can serve as the first step prior to a meeting. You can use them as a form of prework to help determine whether a meeting is needed. By asking everyone to add their comments, questions, ideas, and concerns within the document, you are able to narrow in on the areas that need conversation, which will ultimately save time in the meeting. With this approach, everyone is already on the same page by the time they walk into the meeting.

This approach was used at a meeting I attended with 18 people scattered all over the country. It's hard enough to have a focused, productive virtual meeting, let alone try to work through a document together. We had 20 pages to get through. Rather than wait until we were all on the phone before digging into the material, we shared a Google Doc and encouraged participants to leave comments and questions prior to the meeting. When the meeting began, we already had a basic understanding of who had questions or concerns and on what parts of the document. The review process was significantly faster, and we were able to keep energy up throughout the meeting. There was no time wasted asking, "Who has a question about this?" or "Does anyone want to weigh in here?" The meeting leader already knew the answers and structured the meeting accordingly.

REDUCE AND REPLACE

We often get into the habit of meeting. We have recurring meetings, standing meetings, weekly and even daily meetings, all of which should be questioned. There are many ways to collaborate, even beyond those mentioned above. Shared task systems such as Asana and reporting tools such as 15Five help create transparency and communication flow, which reduce the need for meetings. It's worth exploring what tools and approaches you already use that might be underutilized, as well as what new tools and approaches you can experiment with. The goal is to reduce the number of meetings or time spent in meetings, replace some with an alternative, and completely remove the ones that have no good reason to begin with.

CANCEL IT

Many teams schedule standing meeting times. Some meet weekly or quarterly or take time at the end of every meeting to think about when they're going to meet next. Everyone is usually good at getting meetings on the calendar. Unfortunately, we are not always so good about canceling meetings we don't need.

I heard about a team that had terrible monthly meetings, and when an employee finally confronted the team leader about it by asking what the purpose of the meeting was, the leader replied, "Well, the previous leader was holding them this way, so I thought that's what we were supposed to do." People have meetings for all kinds of reasons. It's time we start to challenge ourselves and others before planning or attending meetings.

If there is no agenda, no desired outcome, and no one thinks the meeting needs to happen, cancel it. Consider the alternative: You will gather everyone into a room to accomplish nothing.

Just because something is on your calendar doesn't mean you need to do it. If the meeting seems unnecessary, speak up. If you don't think you need a real-time conversation, try an alternative. Share a report or an update or ask a few questions by email or chat. Don't meet for those types of needs.

It's everyone's responsibility to make sure the time they spend together is not wasted.

There's a reason the term is "cancellation"—it's "cancel" and "elation" combined. Remember, no one ever complains when a meeting gets canceled.

CHAPTER FIVE REVIEW

- Failure to plan is the "kiss of death" for any meeting. Don't meet unless you know exactly why you're doing it.
- Ask yourself if you even need others to help solve your problem. You might not, or, at the very least, you might not need as many people as you think.
- Don't plan a meeting simply because you feel stuck. Ask yourself a series of questions to determine whether a meeting is the right next step. You might be able to work through things on your own.
- Consider alternatives to meeting. Email, memos, dashboards, shared documents, and chat can save everyone time and aggravation when used appropriately.
- Question every meeting you have. Even if it's a standing meeting you have regularly, it might be unnecessary.
- If it's unnecessary, cancel it or replace it with an alternative format. Everyone will appreciate your consideration and respect of their time.

CHAPTER FIVE ACTION LIST

- How might you use a chat or other tools like 15Five or Asana to reduce the number of meetings needed?
- If you're already using a chat tool, do you have shared practices for how it's to be used? Are your chat rooms structured appropriately? Are people using @ mentions and providing due dates? Consider developing norms or agreements for how your team will use chat together.

- The next time you want to call a meeting, ask yourself these questions to determine whether there's an alternative:
  - Can you send an email or write a memo to share the information?
  - Can you gather input via a shared document using track changes and asking for comments and edits? For visual materials, there are tools such as InVisionApp that allow people to leave comments on images.
  - Can you have the conversation asynchronously via a chat app? Do all the people need to be in the same room at the same time or can they each weigh in over the course of an hour or a day?

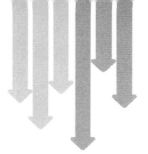

Chapter Six

Desired Outcome

Bad meetings come in many forms, but most can be avoided before you even walk in the door. Consider these very different scenarios of wasteful meetings, all of which could be averted with the same solution.

Scenario One: You grab a seat in the conference room as the rest of the team trickles in for the weekly staff meeting. You start wondering why these meetings happen and how your team leader could still think they're worthwhile after so many seemingly useless ones. Almost without exception, these meetings waste everyone's time. Inevitably, you have something else of greater urgency or importance to do and need just about every minute you can get with it.

Scenario Two: You are invited to a meeting titled "Product Strategy Debrief." *Interesting*, you think. Nothing more is sent, but you're used to that, so you dial into the conference line. A few minutes in, the meeting leader starts talking about what your competitors are doing, the results of the customer survey, and focus groups. People ask questions and a lively discussion ensues.

An hour later, people are packing up. Did you miss something? Sure, it was interesting, but how is this information going to help you do your work?

Scenario Three: You're gathered with a group of people to give feedback on the design of the new marketing campaign. First comes the big reveal, when the marketing team goes through multiple slides and explains how the concept will appear on Facebook, Twitter, your company website, and the e-newsletter. When it's time for feedback, you've got a lot on your mind, but the conversation centers on the second slide and, before you know it, time is up and you haven't gotten to respond to three-quarters of the material. The meeting ends with the promise of another meeting to finish the feedback session.

Do any of these sound familiar?

Yes, these scenarios are beyond frustrating, but take solace. You are not alone in your suffering. I have talked to a number of people who say many of their meetings feel something like this.

Without purpose and structure, a meeting inevitably derails, or perhaps never had tracks to begin with.

There's a reason so many people make the mistake of starting meetings in such vague manners. In most cases, they haven't given enough thought to what they want the meeting to accomplish and whether a meeting is the ideal format for attaining that goal.

The most fundamental and essential element to a productive meeting is the desired outcome. A desired outcome is the specific result you intend the meeting to accomplish. Obviously, if you aren't clear on what you want to accomplish, you have little chance of achieving anything. To determine a meeting's desired outcome, it's helpful to first reflect on why you're having the meeting.

WHAT'S THE REASON FOR THE MEETING?

If you don't have a clear idea of what you want to accomplish from the very beginning, it's nearly impossible to have a successful meeting. Think of it like a compass: If you're one degree off when you start, it might not seem like a big problem, but, after you walk ten miles, you are way off course. If you haven't done the proper preparation to start your meeting off on the right path, it's much harder to have a meaningful, productive conversation.

There are many opportunities to consider the reason for the meeting and articulate it to the participants. Before the meeting, formalizing the purpose helps you plan the agenda and ensure a meeting is the right collaborative approach. Another opportunity comes at the beginning of the meeting when it's crucial to remind all participants why they're there and what the group is going to achieve. Finally, use the follow-through stage to reinforce what the meeting accomplished and to remind all required parties of their responsibilities and tasks. Doing all of this can keep your compass pointed in the right direction.

Meetings without purpose, or that have a purpose not suited for a meeting format, can and should be eliminated from the workplace. We can all agree the most useless waste of time imaginable is to gather a group of people when you don't even know why you're all there.

THE SIX REASONS TO MEET

There are six common reasons to have a meeting. Keep in mind, any one meeting can cover multiple reasons, but often there is a primary purpose. Knowing the high-level reason will help you articulate exactly what you need to accomplish and guide how you structure or design the session.

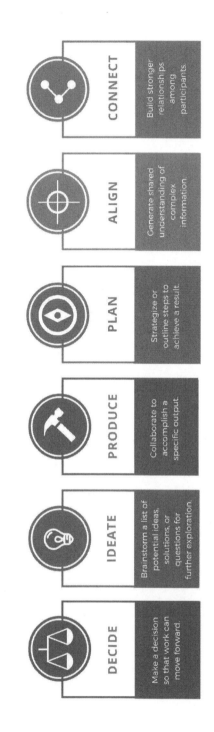

CONNECT — Build stronger relationships among participants.

ALIGN — Generate shared understanding of complex information.

PLAN — Strategize or outline steps to achieve a result.

PRODUCE — Collaborate to accomplish a specific output.

IDEATE — Brainstorm a list of potential ideas, solutions, or questions for further exploration.

DECIDE — Make a decision so that work can move forward.

1. DECIDE

The goal of this meeting is simple and straightforward—you want to come out of it having made one or more decisions. Said decision is clear and understood by the group, so everyone can take the appropriate action.

2. IDEATE

Brainstorming or ideation meetings generate a list of ideas, workable solutions, or questions regarding the matter at hand. These sessions produce lists and options, rather than narrowing down on a single decision.

Brainstorm meetings often go hand in hand with decision meetings where the first part of the agenda is brainstorming and the second part is coming to a decision. In this case, it's a decision-making meeting.

3. PRODUCE

These meetings are often working sessions in which participants create or enhance a deliverable. The resulting material doesn't need to be complete—a work in progress or straw model is completely acceptable. The key is that the outcome is tangible and drives the project forward.

Produce meetings include activities such as creating a brand board, enhancing a strategy document, and composing a customer feedback survey.

4. PLAN

In planning meetings, you establish clear strategies and next steps. Planning meetings can be very detailed, resulting in specific actions ready for you to execute, or high-level, resulting in approaches that will guide the team's work. Use these kinds of meetings to make sure everything is in place to help move your project forward.

5. ALIGN

In alignment meetings, you make sure everyone has a shared understanding of complex information. Everyone talks through the information, situation, or problems and lands on a final shared understanding.

This is different from simply making a presentation, which is rarely a good enough reason to hold a meeting. You are doing more than making sure everyone has the same information. You are both sense-making together and ensuring each person's interpretation of the information is in line with the rest of the group so everyone can move forward on the same page.

6. CONNECT

In this type of meeting, you want to build stronger relationships. These meetings can include team-building exercises, retreat sessions, or involve establishing rapport with a client. No matter the participants, at the end, all parties should feel more connected.

DO NOT MEET FOR "SHARING"

You may have noticed there's not a reason for "sharing" or "presenting" information, because I believe meetings shouldn't be a one-way communication. Meetings that only involve one person talking at the participants are often frustrating and a waste of time. In this case, you can consider other ways to share and present information to your team (read more about meeting alternatives in Chapter Five).

MEETINGS OFTEN HAVE MULTIPLE REASONS

As previously mentioned, though meetings usually have a primary reason, they are rarely limited to only one. Maybe you're having a meeting about making a decision, but you also want to use it as an opportunity to help the team connect. The former objective is external, or what the participants need to know, while the latter is internal, for your own purpose. You won't spell out the internal objective on the agenda, but you can use it to help frame the meeting. It might lead you to make different choices. Perhaps you'll include an introduction that gives people the chance to check in and share differently than if you were just holding a decision-making meeting. Both the internal and external reasons for this meeting are important to the outcomes you want to achieve.

Some meetings also have phases, each of which has its own objective. You might start a decision-making meeting by getting aligned on the information, then have a brainstorming period, and end with the actual decision making. This meeting will be quite different from a decision-making meeting in which three directions are being presented for the group to vote on from the outset. In this second case, the meeting might start with alignment and go right into decision making. Recognizing the multiple phases and objectives of a meeting will help you shape the agenda in preparation for a successful, engaging session.

DEFINING YOUR DESIRED OUTCOME

Once you know the overarching reason for your meeting, you're ready to get specific. Stating that the meeting is to brainstorm ideas is not enough. You need a clear understanding and description of what you intend the meeting to accomplish.

This is a meeting's "desired outcome." A desired outcome is the meeting's end result and a way of measuring whether it was successful or not. By writing a clearly defined desired outcome, you are describing exactly what you expect to come from the meeting. "Begin with the end in mind," as leadership expert Stephen Covey shared in his classic book, *7 Habits of Highly Effective People*. When you can clearly articulate the end results and outputs of a meeting, you're more likely to achieve the outcomes.

Writing a desired outcome can feel time-consuming or even challenging in the beginning, but this is only because you're not yet familiar with the practice. As is the case with learning any new thing, the more you do it, the easier it becomes. Many of Meeteor's clients struggle with desired outcomes at first, but soon find using them in their meetings to be one of the most effective practices they've applied.

Here are a few pointers to getting you started:

START WITH A NOUN, NOT A VERB

Starting with a noun rather than a verb makes it easy to evaluate whether you achieved a specific result. It can be tempting to say the purpose of a meeting is to discuss something or to brainstorm options or to share information. Remind yourself that a purpose is different from an outcome.

We often conflate enjoyable meeting activities with productive ones. It's hard to evaluate whether an activity was useful without knowing what the activity should result in. Imagine reflecting with the team at the end of a meeting and asking, "Did we brainstorm?" That would feel silly. Instead, you might ask, "Did the brainstorm result in what we needed to move forward?" The difference between those two questions is subtle but important.

When you start with a noun, the desired outcome for a brainstorming meeting might be a list of three to five actionable ideas. If, at the end of the meeting, you have no list of ideas or too many wild ideas, you did not achieve your desired outcome. You might have had great conversation and talked through some problems, but without that list of three to five, you missed the mark. You might leave the meeting feeling as if you accomplished something, but in reality, there is still work to be done.

Try using the aforementioned Six Reasons to Meet to frame the outcomes. You might say you want, "A list of next steps for XYZ," "alignment on XYZ," or "decisions on XYZ." Then, you can save the action verbs such as "review," "brainstorm," or "share" for agenda items.

It helps to make the desired outcome specific and avoid using language referring to anything that can't be easily evaluated. In our brainstorming example, "a list of three to five" is better than simply "a list." Taking that further, you might say "a list of three to five ideas to be shared with senior leadership as possible solutions." The addition of the descriptor helps the team evaluate whether the ideas they've selected for the list are appropriate.

LIVE WITH THE AWKWARDNESS

A desired outcome should not be thought of as a goal. A goal is often phrased as a "to" statement. You might say you have a goal to run a marathon. In this case, the outcome is that the marathon was run. That might sound a little awkward, but thinking this way can help you really hone in on what you want to achieve.

Writing things out can help you maintain clarity. Some organizations I've worked with write a purpose statement and an outcome statement. They'll write, "The purpose of the meeting is to review the budget. The outcome is an approved budget." They do this to make sure both are clearly understood by all parties and everyone stays on the same page.

If you're struggling with desired outcomes at first, it might help to give this a try. Start with a "to + verb" statement. Once you've written that, try restating it as a noun by completing the statement, "The outcome of this meeting is..." It might feel strange and the sentence might seem gawky, but it will be much more functional because it will help you hone the foundational need for the meeting. In the process, you'll develop better understanding of the true meaning of a desired outcome and set yourself on the track to better meetings.

For more helpful tools on writing a desired outcome, check out the Resources section at the back of this book and visit www.meeteor.com/momentum/resources.

CALL IT A DESIRED OUTCOME

Language matters. Avoiding confusion and the tendency to make "to + verb" statements is the reason we at Meeteor decided to use the term "outcome" instead of "goal" or "purpose." We try to steer clear of words that can be interpreted in different ways. Focusing on "outcomes" helps you stay crystal clear about both why you are meeting and what you want to achieve. You would never say the outcome of the meeting is a discussion on the budget, yet I've been invited to meetings where the invitation says, "to discuss the updated budget." It's much more useful to say the outcome is "a finalized or approved budget." You go into the meeting intending to leave with a decision: The budget is accepted and can be acted upon. Without that approval, the meeting will not have been a success.

For yourself and others, do your best to consistently use the term "desired outcome." Asking, "Why are we having this meeting?" can be answered in many ways that don't actually clarify what the meeting will accomplish. Instead, ask, "What is the outcome you hope this meeting will achieve?"

This is a surprisingly powerful question. I once was chatting with a woman about her one-on-one meetings with her direct reports. She was complaining that they were not a good use of her time. I first asked why she had them, and her response was, "Because I have to." I quickly realized my question did not produce the answer I was looking for. I asked again in a different way. This time I said, "What do you hope the outcome of a one-on-one will be?" She paused for a moment, then went on to talk herself into all the positive results that can come from a one-on-one: to have stronger relationships with her direct reports, to have problems solved or roadblocks identified so the employee can keep moving, to be more informed about the staffer's workload, etc. This simple reframing enabled her to see these "mandatory" meetings in a new light.

HAVE A DESIRED OUTCOME EVERY TIME

Desired outcomes are crucial to every meeting, including the impromptu ones. Even if you're just having an informal chat, it's important to clarify what you hope to get out of the conversation. It only takes a minute to do, and it will crystallize the reason for the meeting. Any time you interact with a coworker to work through a problem, you must have a clear idea of what you want to accomplish. Otherwise, you risk wasting your time and theirs. Giving yourself just enough of a plan—something along the lines of, "I'm going to show the person this document. What I need is their initial reaction and feedback," or "Here's the question I'm going to ask them"—can help you self-facilitate the conversation and wrap things up quickly. Along the same lines, if a colleague approaches you and asks if you have a few minutes, ask what they need from you before jumping into the conversation.

An impromptu meeting can also take place when a couple of colleagues gather to work things out in a "quick meeting." If you find yourself in this situation, no matter whether you're the meeting leader or a participant, always remember to ask the powerful question, "What is the outcome we hope this meeting will achieve?" It helps everyone to get aligned before the conversation unfolds. If you don't think you can keep things quick, it might be time to consider planning a more formal meeting.

Desired outcomes also are important for marathon meetings that last more than four hours. If the meeting will take place over several hours or days, consider breaking the meeting into mini-sessions, each with their own specific desired outcomes. Sometimes it makes sense to plan one huge meeting where several topics are discussed. In these cases, it helps to treat each of those topics as their own meeting with specific desired outcomes. You might not need to write a complicated agenda for each of the mini-meetings, but being thoughtful about the outcome for each will help ensure the entirety of the time you spend together is productive.

In addition to having a desired outcome for the various sections of your long meeting, it's possible you'll have one general desired outcome for the entire meeting as well. I recently wrote an agenda for a 2-day board meeting with a general desired outcome that all members leave with a deep, rich understanding of the organization's goals, strategies, program areas, and partners. This overarching desired outcome informed how I built out the activities within each topic of the agenda.

INTERNAL AND EXTERNAL DESIRED OUTCOMES

It is possible to have both internal and external desired outcomes for one meeting. The former is something intentionally articulated to the group, whereas the latter might be something only meeting leaders or certain team members need to be cognizant of. If you do have an internal desired outcome or "hidden agenda," be sure to think about how your meeting is designed to achieve that desired outcome, as well as the explicit one.

For example, if you are meeting with a client, the desired outcome written on the agenda might be, "Next steps and revised timeline for this project are agreed upon." Internally, however, your desired outcome might be, "Better understanding of the client's satisfaction with the relationship." You might not write it on the agenda, but it's something for your team to be mindful of.

To accomplish this internal desired outcome, you may pay extra attention to the client's tone or ask them a check-in question about how they're feeling so far about the project. However you address it, you want to leave the meeting with a clear read on the client's satisfaction, as well as agreed-upon next steps and timeline.

USE THE DESIRED OUTCOME TO DETERMINE INVITEES

Ever been to a meeting and wondered why you were there? Including the right people, and only the right people, is critical to the meeting's success. A highly productive meeting can still be a waste of time for someone who didn't have any reason to participate. Therefore, think hard about which colleagues you need and be discerning about who you invite.

The desired outcome will help you distinguish between who needs to attend and who needs to be informed. Consider which individuals have knowledge or perspectives to contribute and those who have authority. Think about which relationships you want to strengthen and whose buy-in you need. The reason for the meeting and the specific desired outcome you write will influence who you invite.

Early on, people might question your choice to only invite a few key people to a meeting. Some people may feel you've intentionally left them out. Yet, at the same time, others may secretly or openly thank you for not taking up time on their calendars, because no one really wants to sit through another meeting just because you felt bad.

If the idea of limiting meeting invites to only the critical contributors seems too outrageous for you or your organization, consider making non-critical participants optional, so they can decide if their attendance is worthwhile. Just be sure to follow up with them and any other stakeholders who need to be kept in the loop so they stay informed of the meeting takeaways.

SHARE THE DESIRED OUTCOME WITH PARTICIPANTS

A desired outcome is not only meant to help you, as the meeting planner. The desired outcome should be shared with meeting participants prior to the meeting, along with the meeting invite and agenda. This will help people determine whether their participation is needed at the meeting and provide confidence that the meeting serves a purpose.

When you receive an invite or agenda without a clear desired outcome, it's your responsibility to ask the meeting leader for more information. Before inquiring, do a bit of reflection and try to estimate what the desired outcome might be. This demonstrates to the meeting leader that you are actively and thoughtfully responding to their meeting invite. You want to avoid coming off as snarky or disapproving of their lack of good process. Instead, you're seeking clarity and providing the leader with a jumping-off point for writing the meeting's desired outcome.

When communicating the desired outcome or asking for one, you can be as formal or as casual as you like. For examples of how to share or request the desired outcome, see Appendix A and check out www.meeteor.com/momentum/resources.

ACCEPT OR DECLINE A MEETING ACCORDINGLY

When you receive an invitation to a meeting, it's important to decide if attending is the right use of your time. The desired outcome provides the first bit of context for this determination. If the meeting leader doesn't provide one, inquire about it. If you can't figure out why you've been invited or what you can contribute, ask for more information. It's imperative we take ownership over our time. Connect with the meeting leader and ask, "Is there something in particular you expect me to contribute to this meeting?" While meeting leaders should be thoughtful about who they invite, they can make mistakes, or, just as likely, they haven't given it enough thought. If you're not convinced your presence is necessary, don't be afraid to say so.

As the meeting leader, let people know it's reasonable for them to opt out of a meeting if they feel it's not the best use of their time. Most workplaces have cultures in which declining a meeting is seen as strange or possibly unacceptable. We should be allowed to decline a meeting for a reason other than a scheduling conflict. To change this dynamic, it's up to the leaders to be clear in letting the team know they can feel free to question their attendance or offer other ways to participate.

Again, it's also acceptable to indicate when attendance is optional. You might note in the invite who needs to be there and who can decide for themselves, based on the agenda. This is helpful when there are people who have a peripheral connection to the content. By doing this, you are giving people permission to say no if they don't feel like it's the right use of their time.

If you need to miss a meeting, Chapter Eleven includes alternative ways to contribute and stay engaged without participating in the actual conversation.

START EACH MEETING WITH THE DESIRED OUTCOME

You spent effort and energy to write the desired outcome—make sure to keep up the great work and use it at the start of your meeting, using it to set the conversation on the right path. It's tempting to jump right in to the conversation, but it's important to get everyone aligned first. I've had times when I'm running from meeting to meeting, and I sit down in a conference room and I'm not even sure which meeting I'm in. Sometimes meetings are set weeks in advance and, by the time the meeting comes around, you can't remember why it was called. As a meeting leader, you cannot assume that because someone showed up at the meeting, they remember or are focused on what this meeting is all about, even though you've shared the desired outcome in advance. It's always a good reminder for everyone gathered to know exactly what you want to accomplish.

Stating the desired outcome at the beginning of the meeting gets everyone mentally prepared for focused work. If you've previously articulated the desired outcome, you might say something like, "The desired outcome of this meeting is (a final version of the deck that is ready to send to the customer). Any suggestions or modifications?" Or, "It would be awesome if we could walk out of this meeting with (a list of 5 critical questions to explore). What do you all think?"

If you are a meeting participant, you can also facilitate the meeting to start with the desired outcome by asking one of the following:

"Can anyone help remind us what we plan to achieve by the end of this meeting?"

"It's my understanding that we'll achieve [alignment on next steps for the marketing campaign] by the end of this meeting. Does this resonate with everyone here?"

"What do we hope we'll get done by the end of this meeting?"

Remember, it's not too late to update a desired outcome at the beginning of a meeting. Things change. When you get into the meeting room, physically or virtually, you might find that the previously agreed-upon desired outcome is no longer appropriate. Don't hesitant to update it before jumping into the conversation.

However you make it happen, you'll find that by getting everyone aligned on what the meeting will achieve will point the conversation down the path to achieve it.

LET THE DESIRED OUTCOME GUIDE CONVERSATION

Though you've shared the desired outcome at the start of the meeting and possibly written it somewhere visible to the whole group, when you're in the middle of an exciting conversation, people can get carried away or the discussion can go off topic. In this case, you can use the desired outcome to reorient the team back to the most important thing at hand. When you notice the meeting has wandered, try asking if this topic will help the group accomplish the desired outcome or if it can be taken off-line.

END WITH THE DESIRED OUTCOME

The meeting is coming to a close, and now's the time to do one final check-in on the desired outcome. Did the group achieve what it set out to? Reflecting on the desired outcome at the end of the meeting helps give closure to the conversation. Many factors contribute to how someone feels about the meeting, but it's especially important to create a sense of accomplishment. Ask the group if you accomplished the desired outcome and what contributed to your success or lack thereof.

Regardless of your role, you can help the team feel a sense of accomplishment and reflect on what could be done differently. At the end of your upcoming meetings, try one of the following questions or statements.

- "What have we achieved in this meeting? What are some immediate next steps?"
- "I noticed we didn't quite achieve what we set out to do in the beginning. I wonder if anyone shares the same feeling. What can we do differently next time?"
- "I'm very glad we achieved [alignment on next steps for the marketing campaign] during today's meeting. Nice work everyone!"

CHAPTER SIX REVIEW

- You must have a reason to meet. Many bad meetings begin with a lack of understanding as to what needs to happen and why.
- There are six reasons to meet: Make a Decision, Brainstorm, Align, Plan, Produce, and Build Relationships. Some meetings have more than one reason.
- A desired outcome is the driving force of any meeting. Be clear when deciding what you want to achieve and use the desired outcome to set the tone and structure of the meeting.
- An "outcome" is different from a "purpose" or a "goal." For example, the purpose of the meeting might be to discuss successful social media campaigns. The outcome of that same meeting is an action plan of how you will implement such tactics into your own strategy.
- You need a desired outcome for every meeting, every time. Even if you're just grabbing a coworker to make a quick decision, go into that exchange knowing exactly what you need. If you're having a marathon meeting, create a desired outcome for every aspect of it.
- Using the desired outcome before, during, and after a meeting helps your team maximize its benefits.
- If you don't know why you're meeting, you probably shouldn't be meeting at all. Be clear in what you want to accomplish before you even begin planning a meeting.

CHAPTER SIX ACTION LIST

- Look at your calendar for the next 1–2 weeks. For each meeting on your calendar, try to state the desired outcome. Keep track of how many meetings fall into each of these categories: (1) I know the desired outcome of this meeting, (2) I have a general sense of the desired outcome, (3) I'm not sure what the desired outcome is.

- For meetings you are leading, try writing a desired outcome(s) for yourself.

- For meetings you are participating in, inquire about the desired outcome from the meeting leader.

- Start a meeting by stating or asking about the desired outcome.

- Keep the desired outcome visible during the meeting and refer to it when needed.

- End a meeting by reflecting on whether you accomplished the desired outcome.

- Visit the Resources section at the back of this book or www. meeteor.com/momentum/resources for additional examples, templates, and support.

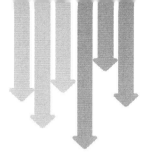

Chapter Seven

Agendas

Once you know why you're meeting, you can begin to plan the rest of the agenda to make sure the desired outcome is achieved. An agenda acts like a roadmap leading you right to your end result. Give it thoughtful consideration and you'll be prepared to reach your destination every time.

COMPONENTS OF AN AGENDA

As mentioned in Chapter Three, a calendar invite is not the same as an agenda. Many agendas consist of a simple bullet point list of topics to discuss. This is a great starting point, but a thoughtful, robust agenda consists of more. The more thought and information you include in your agenda, the more likely you'll have a productive meeting.

A robust agenda includes the following items:

- Desired outcome
- Agenda topics
- Prework
- Norms
- Roles

If you missed the description of desired outcome, go back to Chapter Six.

This chapter is focused on developing the agenda topics as a useful framework for the meeting. Each of the other components have their own chapters, in which we elaborate on how to craft each as part of a thoughtful agenda.

SETTING THE AGENDA

When developing the agenda, start with a list of activities and topics aligned with your desired outcome. Note there are two pieces to an agenda item—the activity and the topic. As you write the list of agenda topics, be as specific as possible. Try to include a verb that describes the activity in addition to the topic of the conversation. For instance, rather than simply writing, "Budget," write, "Review budget" or "Finalize budget."

One word can be confusing. It's understandable why someone might see the word, "Budget" on an agenda and be unsure as to what it means. As a participant, it's much harder to prepare when the agenda is broad or ambiguous. Taking the example further, imagine how you might react differently to an agenda that said, "Review Q4 budget projections and implications," or, "Review YTD (Year-to-Date) budget and answer clarifying questions." The more structure and detail, the better, both for you as the meeting leader and for the participants.

FRAME AGENDA TOPICS AS QUESTIONS

One approach recommended by Roger Schwarz in his *Harvard Business Review* article, "How to Design an Agenda for an Effective Meeting," is to frame the agenda topics as questions. Assigning a question to each topic invites curiosity. It sets a welcoming tone and challenges people to contribute to the conversation. It also helps the group know when the topic is resolved. A general conversation can go on for quite a while, but once a question has been answered, the issue is clearly complete.

Every month at Meeteor, we do an audit review of our social media statistics. The agenda questions might include, "What in this month's report surprised you? What do you find to be confusing? What areas do you think we should pay more attention to?" The next agenda item might focus on ideas for next steps, given the results. Now you ask, "What ideas do you have for building momentum from these successes? What suggestions do you have for things we should stop doing? What recommendations do you have for new things we could do?" A list of questions can elicit engagement and help people enter the conversation. It provides prompts for the facilitator so you never have a moment of silence after asking, "So, who wants to start?"

HOW MUCH TIME DO YOU NEED?

Think of the list of agenda items as the instruction manual for your meeting. When you plan and follow each step, you're more likely to achieve the result you want in the timeframe you've allotted. This last phrase is critical. According to the "planning fallacy," a phenomenon proposed by Daniel Kahneman and Amos Tversky, we consistently underestimate the amount of time something will take. One typical example of this is an opening segment during which each person in the meeting is asked to reflect on the prework, ask questions for clarification, or highlight areas of concern. It might be tempting to allot 5 minutes to this agenda item, but upon further reflection, you realize that with 7 people in the meeting, if each takes 2 minutes, you're suddenly at 14 minutes of reflection. I've sat through many meetings with a jam-packed agenda, only to end up scheduling a follow-up meeting to finish the conversation. Be as accurate as you can when assigning times to all agenda items, including the check-in, and don't feel like you must stick to 5-minute increments. Some things take 2 minutes. Some things take 6. There's no reason to use artificial increments. Thinking through the practical elements and providing estimated times for the specific steps will make sure you're not scheduling too much or too little time to accomplish the meeting's work.

Another common problem is getting stuck on one topic. It's too easy to spend the entire time on the first agenda item and run out of time for the rest, leading to the need for another meeting. But if participants know you only have 10 minutes for this topic, they'll be more likely to keep their comments brief, add value, and stay on topic. When you include the amount of time you intend to spend for each section on the agenda, you are also able to facilitate the conversation to move forward by saying, "We're at the end of the time allotted to this topic. Does anyone have anything new and burning that needs to be shared? If not, let's move on."

Remember, there is no "right" length to a meeting. I recommend you always take the amount of time required to get to the result you need, no matter how long or short that is.

WHO'S LEADING THE DISCUSSION TOPIC?

Sometimes, one person leads the entire meeting, but other times, specific people will present or facilitate individual sections. They are usually the subject matter experts of those agenda topics. For example, at Meeteor, each work-stream leader facilitates the discussion around their respective work stream during our team alignment meetings. This is often a good opportunity for team members to develop their facilitation skills and take ownership of the success of the meeting. You can read more about meeting roles in Chapter Ten and meeting facilitation techniques in Chapter Eleven.

If you want help or if you expect specific people to lead, make sure you communicate your expectations with them and ask them how much time they'll need. Once you confirm these details, you can add their names next to the agenda item they are responsible for, so every meeting participant is clear with the flow.

MUST-HAVE AGENDA ITEMS

A well-structured agenda will always include a few critical activities. We recommend you always begin with a check-in—which brings people into the room and grounds the conversation—and end with a wrap-up to clarify meeting outcomes. More on both practices in Chapter Twelve.

It is important to list "check-in" and "wrap-up" or "check-out" on the agenda for several reasons. First, if you don't list it, you might forget to do it. No matter whether it's in a digital or printed format, your "written" agenda is the physical reminder of what you need to get through. Without seeing "wrap-up" as your last item, you could get caught up in the conversation and forget the wrap-up completely or simply run out of time.

Second, when determining how much time you need for your meeting, you need to have the full picture of your activities. The check-in and wrap-up each often take approximately 5 minutes.

That could be as much as one-third of your meeting time if it's a 30-minute meeting. Forgetting to budget time for those two activities can have a negative impact on how much you accomplish.

Last, by writing them on the agenda, they become official activities, not "nice-to-haves." You can start to build a rhythm or ritual practice others can follow. They see your meetings always start with a check-in and end with a wrap-up. These have been elevated from something one facilitator does to something everyone on the team can do.

MICRO-AGENDA VS. MACRO-AGENDA

You want to keep agendas simple and to-the-point for most of the group, but it's also okay to have a more detailed version for those who need them, such as meeting leaders and facilitators. One company I worked with had what they called a "micro-agenda" and a "macro-agenda." The macro-agenda was sent out to all the participants. It was concise and straightforward, with items written to provide the attendees with enough information to prepare, but not so much to overwhelm. Most of what we've discussed in this chapter so far would be listed in the macro-agenda.

The facilitator would have the micro-agenda, which had much more detailed information. In addition to listing the agenda topics like "Review the Budget (10 minutes, Mamie to lead)," it would include notes like this:

- "Review the Budget (10 minutes, Mamie to lead)
- Review YTD budget document v2
- Call attention to lines 12 (underspend on marketing) and 17 (overspend on consultants)

- Ask for any additional questions for clarification or points to highlight

Doing it this way helps the meeting leader be an effective facilitator without bogging down the rest of the participants with too much information. The leader can refer to their notes rather than tax their brain with recalling all the important points or questions they need in that moment.

Remember, the agenda is a tool meant to make your life easier. Organize it and make it work for you and your team's culture however you see fit.

BUILD THE AGENDA TOGETHER

One way to develop an agenda is to ask participants to suggest topics or issues for discussion. Rather than guessing about what's important or helpful to the group, just ask. You can then prioritize and allot times or ask the topic owner how much time he ideally needs. Rather than leaving sections of the agenda underdeveloped, approach the people driving each topic and let them offer the necessary information.

One of Meeteor's customers in the financial industry established this practice for his staff meeting. He asks everyone on the team to add topics to the agenda before the next meeting. The team leader then prioritizes the topics for the meeting and checks for agreement at the start of the meeting. This approach gives everyone a chance to say, "This is what I need from the team," so the meeting is not just about what the leader needs to get out of that time together.

You might also find that it's more convenient to build the

agenda at the beginning of a meeting rather than send it in advance. This is especially true for impromptu meetings or standing check-in meetings. Often, a brief impromptu meeting doesn't require any agenda topics because the desired outcome is enough. Standing meetings are typically the opposite. If you meet regularly with a colleague or small group to review status updates or multiple projects, it's helpful to take a few minutes at the start of the meeting to develop the agenda together. Talk about what you need to get through and in what order. Write it down so you have a full picture and can prioritize and manage the conversation accordingly.

SEND THE AGENDA AT LEAST 24 HOURS IN ADVANCE

You absolutely must have time to review the agenda prior to the meeting. The agenda helps the participant know if the meeting is an appropriate use of their time and therefore whether she should attend, as well as how to prepare. At least 24 hours in advance, all participants should have the specifics of what the group is expected to accomplish in the meeting. If you are planning the meeting and know exactly what you want to get done, there is no reason to withhold that from those you're inviting. Send all the information up front with the calendar invite to help people determine whether their attendance is truly necessary. Remember to be judicious in who you invite to the meeting. For a refresher on determining who to invite to your meeting, check out Chapter Six.

If, as a meeting participant, you don't receive an agenda 24 hours in advance, you have an obligation to request one, or at least ask, "Can you tell me what you're expecting us to accomplish in this meeting or what role you want me to play?" Participants can play an active role in encouraging planners to create agendas.

BE A PROACTIVE PARTICIPANT

Also as a participant, it's up to you to speak up when things might need to be altered to best serve the group. I was recently invited to a meeting that was supposed to last two hours. We found out close to its start time that two of the critical participants were on a delayed flight, and we had to shift the time to accommodate them. This meant I could only participate in about 45 minutes of the meeting.

I reviewed the agenda and saw not every item required my attention. Rather than sitting in the meeting for the first 45 minutes and only covering a few topics I could contribute to, I pointed out which items pertained most to me and asked if we could rearrange the order to get the best use of my time. My peers were flexible, we switched things up, and we hit every issue that required my participation. They tackled the items less relevant to me after I left, everything got done, and not one minute was wasted.

In some cases, you must be proactive. If I would have just sat through 45 minutes of irrelevant material, it would have been both a disappointment to me and to the meeting leaders who invited me, because they wanted me to weigh in.

HOW TO USE AN AGENDA IN THE MEETING

The power of a thoughtful agenda does not end at the beginning of the meeting. The agenda is there to keep everyone on track. It's an outline meant to keep you moving forward toward your desired outcome. Allow it to do its job by sticking to it as best as you can, while also trying to stay within the established time parameters.

We all have worked with people who like to go off on tangents or keep on talking about a topic once it's already been sufficiently covered. Let the agenda be the bad guy in these cases. Point out when an issue is monopolizing the time, and shut it down. Don't let one part of your meeting steal time from other important matters. If you're not conscious of how a conversation is unfolding, it's easy to let that happen.

You also can grant the facilitator or timekeeper permission to remind the group when it's time to move on. If it's not clear whether it's appropriate to end a conversation, the facilitator can say, "We've run out of time for this topic. Do you all want to keep going? If yes, we'll have to shorten another topic or schedule another meeting." You can also ask if you are missing people or information necessary to completing this conversation. Or, if the conversation has veered too far off topic, it might make more sense to tackle the issue at the end of the meeting. Speak up and say, "I've noticed we've gone off topic. Let's hold this subject and, if we have time at the end of the meeting, we can revisit. But for now, let's get back on track with what was planned for today." Allow yourself the flexibility to table topics not related to the matter at hand by redirecting everyone's attention to the written agenda.

There will also be times when the conversation has gone off track but is clearly critical. There are new or related issues that need to be addressed before going forward. At that point, acknowledge you are off agenda but recommend the group continue down this path because of its critical nature. Make your case and note the change on the existing plan. Pointing out that you're now intentionally straying from the agenda will help the group recognize the difference between unhelpful tangents and useful ones.

HOW TO USE AN AGENDA AT THE END OF A MEETING

When you end your meetings with checking in on the desired outcome, it's also helpful to do a quick review of the agenda topics. Are there any unaddressed items? If so, make sure you have a plan to address them, whether taking it off-line or including it in an upcoming discussion. Are there any next steps you need to capture? Was the allotted time for each agenda item realistic and feasible? If you find you only got through half of the items on your agenda, it's a signal that you might have underestimated the time required for each discussion topic, or you might need to better facilitate and move the conversation along more proactively. Reviewing the agenda at the end and answering the above questions will help you and your team reflect on your time management and meeting design, so you can incorporate these learnings in your future meetings.

CHAPTER SEVEN REVIEW

- Set agenda items to be more descriptive. Rather than "budget review" say "finalize budget." Be as specific as possible.
- Allot specific times for each topic to help you determine whether your agenda is manageable, given the length of your meeting. Time allocations also help you stay on track.
- Use the agenda to push the conversation forward when you get stuck.
- You don't have to do it alone. Assign others specific topics to discuss at the meeting and designate a length of time for each to be covered. Ask for their input when creating the agenda.
- Make time for the check-in and wrap-up.
- Send out the agenda at least 24 hours in advance to give everyone time to review and prepare.
- As a participant, speak up when things change and the agenda needs to reflect that.
- Use the agenda as a guide during the meeting and to measure success at the end. If you've hit every topic and reached your desired outcome, you've succeeded.

CHAPTER SEVEN ACTION LIST

- Look at your calendar for the next 2–3 weeks. If you're leading a meeting, try writing an agenda and share it with meeting participants. If you're attending a meeting, ask the organizer for an agenda.

- For each of the upcoming meetings you're leading, try a different technique or the one that feels most comfortable to you: writing the agenda as questions, creating macro/micro versions, using an activity to increase engagement and keep the energy up.

- When writing a meeting agenda, think about how much time each section will take, who will lead it, and what activity you will do. Consider using a template to remind you to include these elements. Check ours out at www.meeteor.com/momentum/resources.

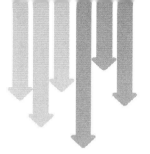

Chapter Eight

Prework

———

Can you imagine what would happen if everyone showed up to a meeting with no idea of what they were there to accomplish? What if no one was prepared to discuss the topics at hand, and everything descended into a disorganized free-for-all? Unfortunately, many of us have experienced this exact scenario. There was no clear prework or no prework at all, so no one came fully prepared to contribute.

Prework is information, prompts, or short assignments distributed to meeting participants in advance of the event. It's designed to help participants prepare for a productive conversation. Prework usually serves two key purposes: First, it provides context and ensures everyone has the same information when they walk into the meeting. This helps optimize the time you have together. You can immediately start the conversation, rather than spend time presenting or sharing information first. Second, it gives participants the freedom to engage with the material when it's most convenient for them. This might be first thing in the morning, when their brain is freshest, or in the afternoon when they have 10 minutes between other things. Not everyone is receptive to listening and immediately responding with brilliant ideas. Additionally, it enables each participant to think ahead of time, so they can reflect on materials and digest information. Research shows that many people do their best thinking 24–48 hours after they've engaged with an idea. This is where the idea of "sleeping on it" originated.

When appropriately designed and assigned, prework can be engaging and beneficial.

THE MANY TYPES OF PREWORK

Prework can take several different forms. It can be a memo or a document. It might be a video the participants should watch or a list of questions they should consider.

Here are a few examples of prework (for more ideas, visit the Appendix):

- Think about the last time you saw a great ad on social media and come prepared to share why it made such an impact.
- Talk to three customers and gather their feedback on the new product packaging.
- Gather information from your department members and come ready to share highlights and current priorities, and any challenges.

Sometimes, you might simply be providing background information related to the meeting, such as reminding participants where the team left off from its last meeting, or of what everyone learned from the last project. In this case, you're asking participants to be informed.

Prework can be more than text, spreadsheets, and charts. I know one CEO who leaves everybody a voice memo as the prework. She talks through the context, provides details, and explains the complexities. Everyone can hear in her voice where she is confident and where she is questioning. If instead she wrote all her thoughts out on paper, the group would not get the richness that comes with being able to hear her voice as she explains everything.

When deciding what prework you'll use, think about your audience and the best format for sharing the information you need them to have. The prework must serve those who will engage with it. This means you might need to create new materials rather than send what you already have. For example, sometimes a spreadsheet is fine; other times converting that spreadsheet into key graphs or charts is better. In some instances, extrapolating information into bullet points is great; other times, writing a case study or a memo to explain information or set context is most effective. There is no one right way. It's up to you to think about the information and the best way to communicate it to your meeting participants.

No matter what approach you choose, try to keep prework straightforward and concise. This greatly increases the chances people will actually do it, which means a smoother meeting and less headaches for you.

HOW TO COMMUNICATE ABOUT PREWORK

If the value of preparing for a meeting is unclear and there are no consequences for failing to do so, prework will naturally fall down people's lists of priorities. If those who do complete it end up feeling like they wasted their time, the cycle is perpetuated. Only when you effectively communicate why the prework is relevant and exactly what people need to do will your team take it seriously.

BE SPECIFIC

Regardless of what the prework is, the meeting leader must offer specific instructions for how participants should approach it. Be clear when communicating what you want them to think about. For example, a prework that reads, "Review the attached document and come ready to share your takeaways and how this will influence your next steps," could yield different results than if it just says, "See attached."

When you provide specific instructions, people can connect how the prework will help the meeting achieve its desired outcomes. It also reduces the human tendency to delay doing work that's not clear.

BE MINDFUL OF PREPARATION TIME

Tell people how much time you expect prework to take. Be realistic in your projection. If you tell them it should take no more than 10 minutes, then send them 65 pages to review, they will likely feel overwhelmed and not even attempt it. A good rule of thumb is to allow for between 5 and 10 minutes of prework for every 30 minutes of meeting.

It's also acceptable in some circumstances to make prework materials optional. One organization I worked with would send out far too much pre-reading—10 or 15 pages for an hour-long meeting. When I told the group about my struggle to read all of it, they explained doing so was unnecessary. Only the first few pages were important. The rest was background information. No one bothered to tell me, and I was frustrated about all the time I'd wasted reading so many pages of detail that didn't actually add to my ability to contribute to the meeting. In this case, the meeting leader had a noble intention: to provide more detailed spreadsheets and background for anyone who wanted it. The problem was that she was unclear in the instructions. This resulted in frustration and wasted time for me because I diligently read all the material. Not everyone takes that approach. For other participants, I imagine they might have stopped doing the prework altogether, feeling overwhelmed by the massive amount of information shared.

When you are mindful of how much time people might spend on doing the prework, you also show you care.

HOW TO INFLUENCE PEOPLE TO DO PREWORK

In an ideal world, everyone would always remember to do the prework without a second thought. Sadly, most people have yet to think of prework with the same respect they give to their other responsibilities. There are ways to encourage meeting participants to prepare, even if you're not in a position of authority.

MAKE IT A TASK

Most of us keep track of our to-do list and are fairly reliable when it comes to completing our tasks. When you start to view prework as a task required for a meeting, you become one step closer to ensuring you complete the prework every time. You can help others develop this mindset with a gentle encouragement. One nonprofit organization I work with has a practice of including a note that instructs people to block time on their calendar to accomplish the prework. This helps create a habit of making prework part of the meeting routine.

REMINDERS MAKE A DIFFERENCE

It helps to send out prework 24-48 hours before meetings. More complex meetings might require prework to be sent out even earlier. If the topic is complicated or the meeting is long, make sure people have plenty of time to do the necessary preparation. When prework is sent more than 48 hours in advance, I recommend you send a reminder the day before or morning of the meeting to make sure everyone remembers to complete it. In the reminder, be sure to include the instructions and materials. Don't make people dig through their email to find your original. That creates an unnecessary obstacle or even an excuse. I've heard people say in a meeting, "I couldn't find the materials so I didn't have a chance to read them."

If this feels like extra work on your end, it doesn't need to be. There are tools that can help automate the process. Outlook and Gmail both have "Send Later" features available so, at the same time you're sending the first email, you can craft the reminder email and tell the system when you want it sent. If the materials are documents and any of the meeting participants have an executive assistant, copy him on the email or separately ask him to print the materials and put them on the person's desk. A stack of papers is a great physical reminder.

SCHEDULE A CHECK-IN

If it's critical that a decision maker or senior leader know certain information before the meeting, schedule a brief time to talk them through the prework. Send a personal message explaining what matters need their specific attention. Request 5-10 minutes of their time, during which you can highlight the key points or elaborate on the concepts, using the materials as your guide.

You don't need to meet with every person prior to the meeting unless it's helpful. I have experienced meetings where everyone came prepared except for the key decision maker. Instead of diving right into the topic, we spent the first few minutes going over the prework. This is not only wasteful and puts time pressure on the rest of the agenda, it also is disrespectful to everyone who came prepared. You can avoid this scenario by having a quick check-in to get any critical participants up to speed.

WHAT IF WE DON'T HAVE TIME FOR PREWORK?

If none of the practices above fit the culture of your organization, some companies, such as Amazon and LinkedIn, include time in the meeting to do the prework. These organizations build time into the agenda to allow for reading several pages that explain everything the group needs to know. This is not a presentation, which runs the risk of becoming too drawn out or spiraling off topic. The materials can be exactly the same as if you sent them ahead of time. They should take no more than 10 minutes at most to consume.

While this is an acceptable solution to a less than ideal situation, it would be much better if everyone did the pre-meeting work expected of them. Finding a quick 10 minutes of your own time to prepare is much better than wasting a shared 10 minutes. Any time you share collectively is precious and worth preserving.

Just think of how much effort goes into scheduling a meeting, especially when senior people with packed days are included. It can be challenging to get 30 minutes when everyone is together. Do you really want to spend a third of that sitting in silence?

PREWORK IS NOT NECESSARY FOR EVERY MEETING

Not all meetings need prework. Remember, prework is just one tool you can use to help participants prepare for the meeting. Think about the nature of your conversation and whether prework can save you time and move the meeting along faster. If nothing seems obvious or relevant, don't force it.

The other reason you might not send prework is if the information is highly sensitive, complex, or needs nuanced explanation. Such content is best kept for in-meeting exploration.

HOW TO USE PREWORK IN MEETINGS

Imagine you are a participant who's spent the time to thoughtfully prepare for the meeting, and when the meeting starts, the meeting leader begins by going through the prework. How frustrating! It's called prework for a reason and should be treated as such.

It's important to create a culture where the value of prework is understood. *We'll go through the document in the meeting anyway, why bother reading it in advance?* the participants might think. Unfortunately, if one person in the group ignores it, the entire meeting can be set back. If everyone is not on the same page from the onset, you might have to waste time going through the material in the meeting. This is particularly problematic if the person who ignored it is a decision maker or someone in a position of authority who either needs the information in order to contribute, or expects you to review it in the meeting—and not doing so would be interpreted as disrespectful. I've seen teams with strong commitments that if no one has done the prework, the meeting is rescheduled. If you're not ready to go that extreme, here are some helpful tips for you to utilize prework during your meetings.

ACKNOWLEDGE THE PREWORK

Be sure to address the prework your team has done and build the meeting's conversation on it. Try to avoid presenting the prework during the meeting unless it's helping the group move the conversation forward. You might want to reference information in the prework, but you don't need to walk through it. In many instances, you only need to be strict about the prework once to drive people to properly prepare. If you, as a meeting leader, let people know you expect them to prepare and there will not be time to review the prework during the meeting, then follow through with that claim. You will likely see a swift change in behavior. It's highly uncomfortable to sit in a meeting without having prepared and realize you're at a disadvantage. If they experience that once or twice in a row, most people will start to take prework seriously.

REINFORCE PREPARATION

Make sure you give positive feedback when team members demonstrate they've done proper preparation by contributing their thoughts based on the prework. You can point this out in different ways. If you're the meeting leader, you might say, "Thank you, Mamie, for pointing that out. That's a great insight from the prework," or, "I'm so glad everyone did the prework so we have time to dive right into the conversation."

If you're a participant, share how the prework helped you contribute to a productive conversation. Try saying at the end of the meeting, "Tai, this prework was really helpful. It gave me the background I needed to participate in today's session." Rewarding desired behavior can reinforce the team to continue the good practice.

ACKNOWLEDGE LACK OF PREPARATION

Where there is a carrot, there can also be a stick. I don't recommend shaming any individual, but you can also help your team understand the difference between meetings in which not all participants completed the prework and meetings where everyone is fully prepared and engaged. As the meeting gets going, ask the group if everyone has read the prework. While occasionally someone might lie to avoid being called out, this bit of peer pressure often will result in people doing proper preparation.

If it becomes clear that people aren't prepared, pause the meeting and acknowledge it. You might say, "Guys, it seems some people didn't do the prework. I feel like it's keeping us from getting the best thinking. I'm concerned that if we go over it now, we won't have time to finish the conversation; but, if we don't, we also won't get the best result." Then give the team the stage to come up with a solution, "So can anyone suggest what would be an appropriate next step?" This can be an uncomfortable conversation. I encourage you to take the risk and bring the issue to the surface so lack of preparation won't become an unending pattern.

Additionally, you can check in with a colleague who consistently comes unprepared. Inquire as to what's hindering her from completing the prework. Sometimes it can be a performance issue, sometimes it's about prioritization, and sometimes it can be misalignment on meeting preparation. Having this conversation demonstrates you value your colleague and see meeting preparation as an essential work responsibility. This conversation gives you the opportunity to restate your expectation that every meeting participant come prepared.

CHAPTER EIGHT REVIEW

- Prework is information, prompts, or short assignments distributed to meeting participants in advance to help them come ready to engage in productive, beneficial conversations.
- Prework can be many things, from documents, to videos, to questions to consider. No matter what it is, it's crucial all participants do it so everyone comes to the meeting on the same page and ready to work.
- The meeting leader must communicate with the team about prework. Send out the materials at least 24–48 before the meeting, include specific instructions, and let everyone know how much time they should devote to it.
- Send reminders or schedule check-ins to help people remember to prepare.
- Check in with key players or decision makers beforehand to make sure they understand the prework.
- Acknowledge the helpfulness of prework during the meeting.
- If no one has done the prework or if certain people never do it, talk about it. It might be awkward in the moment, but it will save you all plenty of wasted time going forward.

CHAPTER EIGHT ACTION LIST

- Do a quick audit of your meetings from last week. How many of them had prework? How many of them could have benefited from prework?
- Take a look at the meetings you're leading next week. What kind of preparation do you want people to do in order to have a more productive conversation? Design prework for an upcoming meeting you're leading. Try not to limit yourself to plain text or documents. See if you can make it fun and engaging.
- Take a look at the meetings you're attending next week. Do you have all the information you need to contribute to the discussion? If you need more context to prepare properly, reach out to the meeting leader for more information.
- Visit the Resources section at the back of this book for a list of formats of prework.

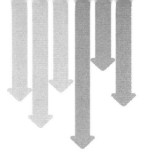

Chapter Nine

Norms

———

Every organization has "a way we do things" that sets the tone for acceptable behaviors within the organization. Employees know certain things are expected of them, and other behaviors simply don't fly. These standards for behavior, whether they are articulated openly on a regular basis or embedded so deeply in the culture they become implicit, are what we call "norms."

Norms are ground rules or guidelines for behavior. They set the foundation for how your team collaborates. They shape how you communicate and interact with one another. When norms are clearly defined and understood by all participants, they can be a powerful tool for moving any meeting forward.

NORMS SUPPORT SHARED UNDERSTANDING AND ALIGNMENT

You may have experienced a moment similar to this: It's your first day at a new job and you're getting ready to head into your first meeting. At your old office, you'd bring your laptop and use it to take notes or search for information as the need arises. You grab your laptop but then pause. Are computers welcome in meetings here? Should you also bring pen and paper, just in case?

This is a simple example of how norms flow through an organization and might not be explicit. It's unlikely the team thought about the pros and cons of having laptops in the meeting. It's more likely no one ever tried to bring a laptop to a meeting, or someone did and was either given dirty looks or outright told to get rid of it. If laptops are commonplace at meetings, it could be that someone brought one and was completely ignored, leaving everyone else to believe laptops must be accepted at meetings. None of these messages are clear or well defined.

This is just one way of illustrating how norms evolve organically and become part of your team culture, whether you agree with them or not. But you can intentionally set norms to create the context for the behaviors you believe will be most helpful.

For example, every brainstorm session has its own parameters and every person has his or her own preferences. If a group gathers to brainstorm and no norms are explicitly in place, some people might throw out wild ideas while others stay strictly conservative. This can potentially lead to judgment, frustration, and poor ideas, leaving some feeling like the session was a waste of time.

The no-boundaries folk will think the more conservative group is thinking too small, not being very creative, or not trying hard to contribute. The conservative folk will think the no-boundaries group is reaching too far, being ridiculous, or not taking the session seriously. In that moment, everyone has different expectations of what the brainstorm should be about. If norms are not specified and agreed to at the start of a meeting, people will act according to their own preferences or what was previously acceptable in this organization's context.

Imagine how these norms would set a very different tone in a brainstorming meeting:

- "When we are brainstorming, all ideas are good ideas."
- "When we are brainstorming, keep budget, time, and resource constraints in mind."

With the first norm, everyone in the meeting knows the group wants to hear as many ideas as possible, both big and small, and there are no boundaries. Conversely, the second norm says clearly only very practical, reasonable ideas are allowed. Only when you establish clear norms and communicate them explicitly can you avoid an unclear situation and get everyone on the same page.

NORMS ENCOURAGE NEW AND UNFAMILIAR BEHAVIORS

Norms are especially powerful for encouraging new or atypical behavior. As a participant, if you're not sure the team or leader will be receptive to your input, you might not act even though you want to. For example, let's say you're acutely aware that one team you're on struggles with staying on topic. Over and over, you watch while the conversation wanders down tangents. If it was your meeting, you'd redirect the conversation back to the agenda. But it's not your meeting and you're uncertain how the group will respond if you step in and facilitate. The leader might feel like you're stepping on his toes or critical of how he runs his meetings. Those engaged in this line of conversation might feel like you're cutting them off. None of those feel like they're worth risking, so, instead, you sit quietly fuming inside.

In this example, the meeting participant is making a judgment about what's best for him and making informed assumptions about the leader and participants. Unfortunately, that means the entire meeting suffers. If only the team had a norm that said, "Recognize when the conversation has wandered off topic and bring the group back to focus," or, "Everyone is responsible for keeping us on track." Then, you've removed some ambiguity from the situation by explicitly stating that anyone can help facilitate. This doesn't mean suddenly everyone will be jumping to cut unhelpful conversation off, but it's a first step down that path.

NORMS REINFORCE DESIRED ORGANIZATIONAL CULTURE

As mentioned, meetings are a microcosm of your organization. How people behave in meetings is also a reflection of your organizational culture. That said, using meeting norms to shape and change behaviors is a way to shape your organization's culture. Over time, meeting norms can permeate other aspects of communication within your organization, shaping behavior beyond meetings. Therefore, when you establish norms, make sure they are aligned with your organizational culture.

For example, if you want an inclusive organizational culture, norms that value all voices should be incorporated in your team meetings. If you are fostering an innovative culture, norms such as "Ask 'How might we?' and think boldly," is a great reinforcement. Norms support culture building by connecting the values you say you want and the practices alive in your meetings.

"NORMS," "GROUND RULES," WHATEVER WORKS FOR YOU

The term "norms" might seem awkward or too professional for

your culture. You don't have to use the term "norms" if it doesn't feel like the right language. We call them norms because if you search the term online, you find an abundance of content specifically related to ground rules of business conduct. This is helpful for finding new norms or gathering ideas for how to use them in your meetings.

If your team doesn't like the word "norms," use something else. "Ground rules" "guidelines," "code of conduct," "rules of engagement," and "expectations" all will work. As long as you are making explicit statements about the kind of behaviors you want for your meeting, they can be called anything you want. Remember, whatever language you select to describe "norms," be consistent, because language is one key component of your organization's culture.

SETTING NORMS

Using norms in your meetings doesn't have to be a big production. Consider starting small and introducing the practice informally. You don't even need to use the words "norms" or "ground rules." Just verbalize your hopes for the meeting. You can say, "I hope everyone will help keep us on track as we have such a full agenda," or, "I'd like everyone to reserve judgment during brainstorming until all the ideas have been shared." Simply externalizing how you'd like participants to behave can be enough to get you going.

The easiest way to get started is to work from a list of existing norms. Check out ours at www.meeteor.com/momentum/resources. You can select norms on your own and share them informally, or provide your team a list and ask them to choose the ones most relevant to the team overall or a particular meeting.

Try asking the group, "Which of the ground rules listed on this sheet would you like to suggest we follow for today's discussion?"

Alternatively, you can create your own norms alone or together. If you can't find a norm that fits your need, write one. If handing out a list of norms in a meeting feels strange, ask the group to identify guidelines that will help the conversation be most productive. In this case, it's helpful to share one or two as examples, but most teams are able to quickly identify a handful of norms.

Once your team gets used to having and referencing norms in your meetings, you might find that you have standing norms and revolving norms. Standing norms become the culture of your team and meetings. You don't need to write them on every agenda or read them aloud at the start of every meeting because they are now "how things are done around here." Just be aware that when a new person joins your team or meetings, they will experience these norms as implicit and will need to be oriented to them.

The norms you explicitly state at every meeting will be those that either fit the specific circumstances of that meeting, such as how the group will approach brainstorming, or be practices you want people to keep top of mind, such as sharing alternative and dissenting perspectives to challenge thinking. If you read all the norms aloud at every meeting, you could end up with not enough time for the conversation or too many ground rules to manage. Instead, focus on no more than five you really want to emphasize.

TEAM BUY-IN IS ESSENTIAL

When everyone is involved in co-creating the meeting norms, they tend to feel more ownership over the process and end result. Setting norms together as a team makes them more powerful and likely to have a lasting effect. Meeting norms owned by the team aren't just one person's idea and are therefore easier to reinforce. As leadership consultant Roger Schwarz shared in his article, "8 Ground Rules for Great Meetings" in *Harvard Business Review*, "A set of behaviors aren't your team's ground rules until everyone on the team agrees to use them."

One way to generate buy-in is to have the team craft norms from scratch and write them in a way that reflects the uniqueness of the team. Norms that use familiar language, inside jokes, or other team-centric concepts can be more palatable. For example, one team I know uses the norm, "Don't make Pesach." Pesach is the Jewish holiday Passover. To "make Pesach" is to make things more complicated than they need to be. For this team, the shorthand "Don't make Pesach" feels more authentic than "Keep things simple" or "Don't overcomplicate matters."

Another example is from one of Meeteor's customers at a nonprofit organization. This organization has a norm of starting the conversation by "going up to the balcony" and then "going down to the orchestra." This theater reference directs people to mentally start the conversation with big-picture thinking and then signals when it's time to zoom in on the details.

To create your own norms, take some time as a group to reflect on the meeting behaviors that would help make your meetings more productive and the values the team wants to uphold. Then ask everyone to write possible norms on Post-it notes or a shared document for the team to use as a discussion launching point. No matter how you start settings norms in your meetings, you need to get your team's involvement, agreement, and commitment.

EXAMPLES OF NORMS

Not all situations require the same behaviors, and it's useful to establish ground rules based on the type of discussion or meeting. Clear meeting norms will align the participants' expectations and guide the actions of team members so you can have a more productive discussion. There are many norms that work in a variety of different scenarios. Some norms, such as those that refer to processes, preparation, and communication practices, can apply to any meeting. Other norms, such as those specific to brainstorming or decision making, work best in certain settings. The following are just a few examples of the norms we use at Meeteor.

For more norms, check out the list we've compiled of process norms, brainstorming norms, preparation norms, as well as norms for specific types of meetings. Visit www.meeteor.com/momentum/resources to download.

READ THE AGENDA AND DO PREWORK AHEAD OF TIME

By the time you're reading this chapter, this norm might seem very straightforward. Of course, we want everyone to come ready to engage in the conversation, so proper preparation is essential. Although this is a standard expectation, we always want to remind people we take prework seriously. If your team doesn't have this habit yet, including this norm on the agenda will create a friendly cue that it's a process norm.

ASK QUESTIONS FOR CLARIFICATION

We never want people to feel like they can't ask a question because they don't want to look stupid or feel bad. We strive to make our meetings a safe space for people to ask any kind of question. Furthermore, asking for clarification also helps people avoid making assumptions, which can cause all sorts of challenges.

KEEP COMMENTS BRIEF AND TO THE POINT

When we're sharing a lot of information about different work streams, we don't need people to go on and on. In most cases, we've already shared most of the information in a Google Doc ahead of time. Elaboration is fine, but comments are expected to remain brief.

AIM FOR GETGO—GOOD ENOUGH TO GO—NOT PERFECTION

We've seen how easily we can get caught up in making the perfect decision or producing the best solution. "Good enough to go," or "GETGO," is a phrase we use at Meeteor to make the call to move work forward, even if the work is not 100 percent. We're able to ask, "Is this GETGO?" and assess whether spending more time on the work at hand is worthwhile. GETGO relieves us from the pressure of having to produce "perfect" work and reminds us to pursue our top priorities.

USE "YES, AND…"; AVOID "NO, BUT…"

This norm is inspired by a practice originated in improvisational theater. It encourages participants to build on each other's idea instead of judging or rejecting ideas different from their own. We often employ this norm in our brainstorming meetings. When someone responds to an idea with, "I don't think that will work because…," we can interject and say something like, "Hold on. Can you rephrase that as 'Yes, and…'?"

PLAY DEVIL'S ADVOCATE

One of our favorite norms is "play devil's advocate," because it gives permission to ask the tough questions and push back on ideas. This has become common practice at Meeteor, but that's not the case on every team. Surfacing opposing viewpoints can be uncomfortable. For some teams, going against a boss or arguing with a colleague might be seen as stepping out of line or not being a team player. Use a norm like this one to create a culture where alternative thinking is welcome.

Even with this norm explicitly stated, it can be one of the more challenging to implement. If no one is actively playing devil's advocate, it's important for the meeting facilitator to invite this behavior more directly. You might say, "I haven't heard anybody play devil's advocate yet. Let's all give it a try. For the next 3 minutes, let's only share reasons why this is a bad decision." This gives people who might be tentative about sharing a conflicting idea or asking a tough question permission to do so.

NORMS FOR DECISION-MAKING MEETINGS

When you're running a decision-making meeting, it's helpful to define norms specifically based on how you'll make the decision and how people should behave once the decision is made. Here are some common ones:

WE WILL USE [CONSENSUS, CONSULTATIVE, MAJORITY RULE, SINGLE DECIDER] AS OUR DECISION-MAKING PROCESS

Knowing how the decision will be made is helpful for everyone. As a meeting leader, it helps me be thoughtful about who should be part of the decision-making process and in what ways. As a participant, it avoids frustration that can arise from unmet expectations. I've had the unfortunate experience of entering a meeting with the assumption the decision will be made by consensus, only to watch the leader decide unilaterally. This almost never leaves participants with a positive feeling, regardless of whether they agreed with the final decision.

EACH PERSON IS RESPONSIBLE FOR ENSURING THEY UNDERSTAND THE OPTIONS AND ARGUMENTS BEFORE DECIDING

I've seen teams start the voting process before everyone clearly understands the options. Then, after the meeting, and as people learn more about the options, some want to change their position. This can happen when a team feels rushed to make a decision, when someone feels uncomfortable or is worried about looking stupid when asking for more information, or when the leader doesn't encourage discussion on the options.

With this norm, each person is responsible for raising questions when they still need more information. This puts the onus on the individual to speak up and reminds the leader that spending time to discuss options is important.

BE WILLING TO SUPPORT A TEAM CONSENSUS EVEN IF YOU DON'T INITIALLY AGREE WITH IT

When you make decisions by consensus, or any other method, it's possible people will still hold on to their ideas or other options too tightly. Some might even try to prove their idea, which wasn't selected as the "right" one. Not only is that counterproductive, but it can also be hurtful to the team dynamic. This norm attempts to garner public support or at least minimize the chance that someone will try to undermine a decision. It's important for people to recognize they need to move on and separate their own personal feelings from what's best for the team. For even greater emphasis, you can couple this norm with, "Don't continue to push your ideas after a decision has been made."

NORMS FOR VIRTUAL MEETINGS

With team members in five different countries, most of our meetings at Meeteor are virtual. There are a couple of technical-related norms we consistently apply. Over time, they have become habit, and we don't include them on the agenda anymore.

TURN ON YOUR VIDEO WHENEVER POSSIBLE

There is a significant difference in the level of engagement in an audio conference versus a video conference. We encourage people to turn on their video whenever possible, knowing that sometimes Internet bandwidth inhibits use of video. It's always nice to see the faces of our remote colleagues, and video helps us maintain a personal connection.

FOLLOW AN ORGANIZED LINEUP TO ENSURE EACH PERSON HAS A CHANCE TO RESPOND

When some of your colleagues are co-located and some are remote, people who have dialed in can have difficulty chiming in. This is true when everyone is calling in as well. When you establish a process for a virtual round-robin, everyone knows there will be time for them to contribute to the conversation, and you'll be sure not to miss anyone or surprise them by calling their name.

USE THE MUTE BUTTON WHEN YOU'RE NOT SPEAKING

Nothing is more annoying on a conference call than random squeaking or typing in the background. Too many minutes are spent trying to find the source of that disturbing background noise. To prevent this unpleasant experience, gently remind each other to use the mute button and prevent the transmission of background noise.

INCLUDE MEETING NORMS IN YOUR AGENDA

Meeting norms are another way to help participants prepare for the conversation. Set expectations ahead of time so people have a chance to acclimate to the type of conversation they are going to have. You can include them in the agenda itself or in an email message about the meeting.

USING NORMS DURING THE MEETING

Norms are one tool you can employ to facilitate the conversation toward a productive outcome. To help yourself and others follow the norms, you need to frame the conversation so everyone is reminded of what's expected of them. Once everyone is clear, you can leverage the norms to guide behavior.

REVIEW NORMS AT THE BEGINNING

Just like the desired outcome, a refresher at the start of the meeting will ensure people are aware of the ground rules for the ensuing conversation. Just because you listed them on the agenda doesn't mean people will remember them.

When you acknowledge the norms at the beginning of your meeting, it's easier to refer to them later on. It can be the difference between trying to find a polite way to tell James he's been hogging the microphone—and you really want to hear from other people—and simply saying, "One of our norms for this meeting was to balance participation. I want to make sure we give time for our colleagues who haven't spoken yet to share their ideas."

You can present the norms as a list and read each aloud or casually comment on how you hope people will act. Either way, the goal is to eliminate any excuses for unhelpful behavior.

GET COMMITMENT FROM THE TEAM

In some cases, getting verbal commitment from the group up front can be helpful. If you want people to follow certain behaviors, especially new or uncomfortable ones, getting them to commit up front is a powerful influence. Writing them on the agenda doesn't necessarily mean everybody is agreeing to them. Remind everyone of their importance and ask for buy-in.

I do this by saying, "These are the norms I'm proposing. Does everybody agree to these? Does anyone want to suggest any modifications or have anything else to add to our list of norms?" It's a way of getting the whole group to collectively accept the norms in preparation of holding one another accountable.

This is particularly important when the norms are slightly different from what your group is used to, or when you have certain people who are constantly behaving in opposition to the norms. Verbal agreement to uphold the norms is an effective initial step to start changing behavior.

KEEP NORMS VISIBLE

It's great to include the norms in the agenda you have in front of you during the meeting, but even still, it's not easy to remember all of them throughout the meeting. Write your norms on a whiteboard or flip chart, or project them on the screen so they serve as a visual reminder to the entire group. This makes it easier for the group to remember the norms as the conversation flows and people can check their own behavior during the meeting.

EVERYONE CAN ACKNOWLEDGE WHEN NORMS ARE NOT FOLLOWED

If the team doesn't uphold these norms, it doesn't matter that you've done the work of creating them. In fact, it might even be harmful to have norms that you allow everyone to ignore, because you've inadvertently demonstrated you are unwilling to do the work of leading the team to what you believe is a more desirable, productive culture.

That being said, you should not rely on the leader or any one person alone to identify whether people are following or violating the norms. To help with this, we use a norm of "Everyone is responsible for upholding the norms. Acknowledge if you notice we are not doing so." It encourages everyone to follow the norms and empowers them to call out when norms are not followed, so it's not just the meeting leader's responsibility. If people don't feel like they have permission or authority to speak up when a colleague is ignoring a norm, they might not. Then, instead of removing or reducing the unhelpful behavior, the individual is sitting there annoyed that someone isn't following a norm and frustrated that the leader isn't doing anything about it.

MAKE NORMS THE "BAD GUY"

Relying on norms lets you guide or redirect behavior without "being the bad guy." For example, I was in a meeting where we agreed not to offer advice but only ask questions to advance the thinking. It was part of a problem-solving meeting, but this portion was only focused on deepening our understanding of the problem and helping the speaker surface their own solutions.

At one point, someone started describing the solution he used when he faced a similar problem in his work. Shortly after he began, one person jumped in to cut him off. She said, "Thanks, Gary, but I want to remind you that we agreed not to give advice during this session. If you want to share your experience with Priya later, you can discuss that with her another time." While it's not always easy to interrupt someone, it helps when you've got a norm to fall back on.

Calling someone out doesn't have to be confrontational. You can use a gentle nudge that doesn't even mention the person's name. For example, if people are talking over each other, remind them of the norm to let one person talk at a time. Say something like, "I'm hearing a lot of interrupting and we agreed to let one person talk at a time. Why don't we go around the table so we each get a chance to share our thoughts and be heard?"

USE NORMS TO EMPOWER YOURSELF

Norms can embolden your own behavior in meetings. If you want to offer an idea that challenges the group's perspective, bring up the norm of playing devil's advocate. You can say, "We agreed people should play devil's advocate, so I'd like to offer some controversial ideas." Same goes for keeping the conversation on track. A friendly mention of a norm can ease your way into facilitating the conversation when you're a participant. "I'm noticing this conversation has wandered off the topic. Can we put it on the back burner so we have time to get through the topics on the agenda that need our attention?"

CELEBRATE WHEN PEOPLE FOLLOW THE NORMS

One way to encourage continued adherence to the norms is to celebrate when people follow and employ them. A simple "thank you" when someone calls upon a norm can go a long way. Demonstrate public appreciation for the person who took the risk and did what you asked of him. You can also celebrate at the end of the meeting. Point out how the group did a great job of following the norms and the impact you think it had on the quality of the meeting. For example, maybe you got through the whole agenda because everyone came prepared or you put tangential topics in the parking lot. Maybe you got a list of great ideas because everyone refrained from judging. The more you emphasize the value of norms, the easier it will be for others to adopt them.

CHAPTER NINE REVIEW

- Norms are guidelines for behavior. They let everyone in the organization know what is expected and what will not be tolerated in the meeting environment.
- You can set norms to remove ambiguity and elicit desired behavior from the group.
- Norms can be anything you want them to be, as long as they are enforced and accepted by everyone in the group. You also can call them whatever you want, as long as it's in keeping with language your team is comfortable with.
- Create norms as a group to increase buy-in and give everyone ownership over them.
- Set specific norms for virtual meetings to avoid technical distractions and help everyone feel engaged.
- If need be, write norms right on the agenda to remind everyone of them. You can also get people to verbally commit to norms at the beginning of the meeting to start everyone off on the right foot.
- Everyone should be responsible for holding one another accountable when it comes to adhering to norms.
- If people aren't following norms, say so. If they are, celebrate it!

CHAPTER NINE ACTION LIST

- Think about your brainstorming, decision making, alignment, and other types of meetings. Ask yourself:
  - Which of these meetings would benefit from norms that promote a different kind of behavior than what is currently happening?
  - Are there meetings that suffer from challenging situations or behaviors such as lack of structure, not starting or ending on time, dominant participants, interruptions, or getting sidetracked?
- Reference the list of sample norms in the Resource section at the end of this book or on our website at www.meeteor.com/momentum/resources. Pick one or two to use informally with your team. Suggest the behavior without calling it a norm.
- Introduce the concept of norms to your team. Share a list of norms and ask them to pick the ones that resonate with them to try during the meeting.
- Reflect on your own behavior and your willingness to call out behavior in conflict with the agreed-upon norms.

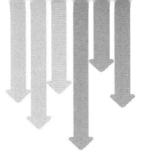

Chapter Ten

Meeting Roles

———

Meeting leaders often feel overwhelmed during meetings as various obligations compete for their attention—facilitating the conversation, engaging people, keeping the conversation on track, monitoring the time, and taking clear and actionable notes. It's one of the most frequently asked questions from our customers: How can one manage to hold a productive meeting, but also stay sane during the process?

DON'T TRY TO BE A MEETING HERO

In a time-sensitive and highly stressful activity like meetings, we can easily fall into the trap of feeling like we need to do it all. As management guru Margaret Wheatley says, "Leadership is a series of behaviors rather than a role for heroes." While it seems like an incredible feat, it doesn't take heroics to lead a successful meeting. Put aside your image of an effective meeting leader as one who can successfully multitask. Instead, take a step back to reflect on what resources you have at your disposal that can help you to run an effective and successful meeting. Look around, especially at the team you're meeting with. They are the power of your meeting engine. You just need to leverage them to help manage the meeting process and achieve greater outcomes.

TYPES OF ROLES

To benefit from sharing the meeting responsibilities, it's helpful to establish meeting roles and assign them. Without clearly defined meeting roles, it's hard for people to know exactly what actions to take to fulfill their role and support the meeting's success. When the roles are not assigned, the burden of doing all the work may fall to one person, or key meeting tasks like note-taking or time management simply don't get done. Here are some common roles that help meetings function more effectively.

LEADER

Meeting leader may seem like an obvious role, but it's worthwhile to take a moment to define exactly what this position is all about. The meeting leader is responsible for calling the meeting, setting the agenda, and ensuring proper preparation. The leader is often held responsible for the success or failure of the meeting. Participants look to the leader as the person in charge, regardless of whether she is the most senior person in the meeting.

In many cases, the meeting leader is also playing every other role. It can be hard to untangle the leader role from the facilitator, timekeeper, and other roles, but they are separate responsibilities. As the meeting leader, your task is to ensure all the other roles are addressed, either by assigning them or doing them yourself, which sometimes is the only option.

There can also be topic or activity leaders who take over during specific portions of the agenda. Empowering others to lead is a fantastic way to share responsibility and provides opportunities for others to grow.

FACILITATOR

The facilitator guides the group through the agenda, keeps everyone engaged and the conversation on track, and makes sure the norms are employed, all with the purpose of moving the team toward a common goal.

The facilitator doesn't need to be the formal leader of the group, nor an expert in the content—the "what" of the meeting. Sometimes she doesn't even need to be a member of the group, such as in the case of a consultant stepping in to mediate a dispute. Instead, the facilitator is in charge of the meeting process—"how" the meeting will progress through the agenda topics.

This is why some teams bring in outside facilitators. They can devote their full attention to keeping the conversation on track, ensuring norms are being followed, and managing the group dynamic. These people don't need to know about the content, they just need to know the process—how to ask questions, elicit feedback, help surface assumptions, and make sure everyone is heard. This allows the entire team to focus on the content. You don't always need to hire a professional facilitator. If you know of someone who is skilled in facilitation, ask if he's willing to facilitate meetings for teams other than his own.

The facilitator's responsibilities can be shared among all participants, but having a single person who's assigned to keep a special eye out is still recommended. Yes, the whole group should be calling on norms and paying attention to when the conversation wanders, but sometimes when everyone is responsible, no one is. Appointing one person to be the facilitator can empower him to speak up and call a disruptive behavior out because "it's my job." You do run the risk of other's not stepping up because they haven't been asked to be the official facilitator of the meeting, so you'll want to reiterate that everyone is still responsible for upholding the norms and keeping the conversation on track. The facilitator is just paying extra attention to these things to support the meeting's success.

Everyone on your team has the potential to become an effective facilitator. A skilled facilitator fosters collaboration and teamwork and manages conflict among team members. She recognizes the dynamics of the group and asks questions to bring out ideas from others. She's not at the center of the stage; instead, she creates opportunities for the participants to shine. She actively listens to the participants, synthesizes the comments, and frames the conversation. She moves the participants along the agenda and helps achieve the meeting's desired outcome. To learn more about different engagement strategies a facilitator can apply, read Chapter Eleven.

NOTE-TAKER

Many people think of note-taking as an administrative task, but it's actually a skill that, done thoughtfully, requires active attention and critical thinking. In many ways, note-takers can be as powerful as facilitators when it comes to helping the team achieve the desired outcome. They play an important role in both keeping the conversation on track and producing something valuable past the end of the meeting.

Note-takers keep everyone on the same page and provide clarity by leveraging their need to capture the conversation. When you're tasked with writing down tasks, decisions, and learnings, you need them to be both clear and accurate. As a note-taker, you have permission to ask the group to pause and spend a moment crystallizing the discussion or fleshing out an agreement. When you do this, you're helping the team refine their thinking, as well as aiding the facilitator to move the discussion forward.

I've done this in many meetings when the decision or task wasn't completely clear. That moment of, "Okay, so we all agree. Let's move on," can lead to ambiguous notes. This is your opportunity to jump in and say, "Great! Can someone restate the decision so I can make sure I've captured it accurately?" You don't need to be the one to always synthesize the conversation and extrapolate the takeaway. Use your fellow meeting participants to recap or restate the important information. Your job as a note-taker is to notice when you need to call the question to ask, "Who is going to follow up with Sherry about the updated timeline?"

The second part of the note-taker role is to advance the conversation when the group is circling an issue or decision. Sometimes, the conversation gets stuck and it's unclear what options are on the table and where the group is heading. Instead of letting the discussion go on and on, the note-taker can propose someone restate where the situation stands. What options are being considered? What are the pros and cons of each? Sometimes, simply summarizing the conversation helps people find clarity and alignment.

This has been the case in a few meetings I've attended where one participant called it "violent agreement." We're so deep into the discussion that we've run past the decision. He states the decision "for the record" and, when we all approve, it's clear we're so engaged that we don't notice we've already come to agreement.

When you observe the group struggling to move things forward, you might say, "I'm trying to capture this correctly. Can someone state the current options we're considering?" Or, "I think the group is nearing a decision. Would someone mind stating it for the record and we can see if that accurately captures it?" This can both help the team stay on track and help you make sure the notes correctly reflect the conversation. If you don't understand what the decision was, you have a responsibly to get clarification and, in doing so, make sure everyone is on the same page.

At the end of the meeting, the note-taker can quickly go through the notes, highlighting important decisions, key takeaways, and next steps to get everyone's final approval or feedback. This is especially important if your team has someone who's not a participant join the meeting specifically to take notes. The benefit of allowing all meeting attendants to be fully engaged in the conversation is invaluable, but it can be tricky for an "outsider" to always capture the notes correctly. Use a few minutes at the end of the meeting to ensure the decisions are recorded accurately and each action has been assigned an owner who will be responsible for completing it.

Ideally, when the meeting concludes, the notes have been informally approved by the group and can be immediately shared. Be sure to consider who needs to receive the meeting notes. There are often stakeholders who did not participate in the meeting but who need to be kept informed. If you've captured notes by hand, you're responsible for ensuring they are captured digitally and stored in a way that the group can access them when needed.

TIMEKEEPER

When your meeting is packed with multiple agenda items, it's critical to keep an eye on the clock. Generally, this responsibility falls to the leader or facilitator, but it's also an easy task to delegate. Timekeepers remind the group when it's time to move forward or alert the group that time is running out. If you worry about cutting conversation off, there are a variety of ways to interject without forcing the group to end abruptly. Consider using one of these approaches:

- "I just want to remind everyone we've only allotted 10 minutes for this conversation, so please keep your comments brief and to the point."
- "Head's up—we've got 2 minutes left for this discussion. Is there anything new or burning that someone wants to add before we wrap up?"
- "We've reached the end of the time for this topic. It seems like we might not be ready to move on. Would you like to stay on this topic for another 5 minutes and cut that time from somewhere else, or should we move on?"
- "Time check—we're nearing the end our time. Does anyone who hasn't spoken yet have something to add?"
- "Sorry for the interruption, but I want to make sure we have time for the rest of the topics on the agenda. Is it okay if we continue this conversation off-line so we can move to the next topic?"
- "As timekeeper, I want to be sure to keep on track. Any final thoughts before we move on?"

When you're the timekeeper, you act like a partner to the

facilitator. As a formal role, you not only have the authority, but also the obligation to interrupt a conversation to help the facilitator manage the group.

No one wants to be looking at his or her watch all the time. It's distracting to the timekeeper and everyone else in the room. There may also be times when you don't feel comfortable interrupting the conversation verbally. For all these reasons, I recommend setting an alarm to help you keep within the time boundaries you've set. You still need a timekeeper to be responsible for the alarm. She can decide whether she prefers to set the alarm on vibrate and verbally notify the group of time constraints or set it with an audible tone so the alarm is the initial interrupter.

TECHNOLOGY KEEPER

Technology has become part of almost every meeting. Unfortunately, many meetings begin something like this: You're scheduled to hold a virtual meeting, but the meeting participant who normally sets up the calls is running late. Nobody knows the leader pin code so precious minutes go by while you're all waiting on the line listening to beeps. Or, no one knows how to set up the projector in this meeting room so you call the IT department and request they send someone. You wait a minute and then start the meeting somewhat hesitantly before being interrupted when the IT guy finally arrives. Or, you click the link in the calendar invite and can't get your video to work. It keeps freezing and the audio is choppy. There is discussion of hanging up and calling back in or switching to a different service. It's hard to follow what to do because you can't hear well. Do any of these sound familiar to you?

With all the benefits of technology, there are still plenty of drawbacks. It's important to designate someone to set up any necessary technology for the meeting. This person needs to be responsible for connecting computers to projectors, ensuring participants have the right dial-in information or link, and informing participants when something goes wrong. This could mean sending people the new conference line information or texting a fellow participant the leader pin if he's running behind. When you don't have a point person to keep your technology under control, you risk wasting time at the beginning of a meeting and losing everyone's attention before you even have a chance to gain it.

PARTICIPANTS

Typically, everyone in the meeting has the role of "participant." As a participant, think about what value or ideas you can contribute to the meeting. Sometimes, you're asked to come because you have a unique perspective or specific advice to share. You might be a decision maker. You might have information the group needs to move forward. Whatever is required of you, be prepared to offer it to the group.

As a participant, you can offer to support the meeting leader by suggesting you keep time, take notes, or help facilitate. Even without taking on a formal role, you can use the techniques previously described to foster a more productive meeting.

OTHER ROLES

The preceding examples are just a few of the possible meeting roles, and they are mostly functional roles. As a team, you can create any roles you want. Some teams assign a scribe who captures key takeaways on the whiteboard, a flip chart, or a shared screen in the moment. Some companies choose to assign the role of devil's advocate to a specific person, rather than have it as a norm for the entire group. I've seen teams with one person who's assigned to identify and capture back-burner items and other specialty activities.

WHY YOU SHOULD ROTATE MEETING ROLES

Rotating meeting roles and responsibilities among all team members can shift a stuck or unproductive dynamic and create a more positive team culture. Team members can develop new skills, feel accountable for the meeting's success, and strengthen the bond with one another.

SKILL BUILDING

Planning a meeting agenda, facilitating a meeting, and taking meeting notes are helpful tools for almost everyone. Creating a meeting agenda builds critical thinking skills. You need to identify a meeting's desired outcome and design the path to reach it. Facilitating a meeting develops leadership skills like active listening and asking the right questions to elicit information. Capturing effective meeting notes practices listening, distilling information, and organizing skills. One of the fastest ways to pick up new skills is to learn by doing. Why not learn by taking on the various roles that make meetings successful?

OWNERSHIP

Rotating meeting roles increases the likelihood that team members feel ownership in the meeting's success. They may even feel empowered to challenge the status quo about how meetings are run. For example, once you've experienced the process of taking notes, you may come up with an alternative approach to note-taking that will make your meetings even more effective.

STRONGER RELATIONSHIPS

Trying different meeting roles helps the team build stronger relationships through empathy. It's much easier to relate to someone when you have a shared experience. You can learn from each person's style and gain a greater understanding of one another. For example, you might not realize how challenging note-taking is until you are assigned to do it. Suddenly, you have a whole new appreciation for your colleague who's been taking notes for the past six months.

Rotating roles might not make sense for smaller teams, and in some cases, the ability to do it depends on the capabilities of the members. If you have a skilled facilitator or note-taker on your team, take advantage of it. Find the right balance between rotating and enabling people to leverage their skills.

When you decided to rotate meeting roles, anticipate a learning curve. It takes time and practice for team members to learn the new skills, feel comfortable in new roles, and be as effective as possible. Depending on the readiness of your team, start small with one or two roles like the note-taker or timekeeper. Or, have more experienced team members mentor others who take on new meeting roles. Consider making developing facilitation skill a professional development goal.

HOW TO ASSIGN MEETING ROLES

Roles can be assigned through a number of approaches:

- The meeting leader can assign roles.
- The meeting leader can ask people to volunteer for roles.
- Your team can have a standing practice of rotating roles.
- People can pick roles out of a hat.
- Your team can have "informal" or "habitual" roles.

If you as the leader are assigning roles, be thoughtful of how you dole them out. In most cases, you don't want to always make the same people take on the same roles. You should also be sure to thank people for taking their role seriously and contributing to the meeting's success.

You can also ask people to volunteer for roles. This lets people feel like they are opting in rather than being told what to do, which gives them more ownership over the role. When doing this, it's still important to avoid letting the same person volunteer for the same task every time. If you notice a pattern, jump in and say, "Rachel has been the timekeeper for the past few meetings. Can someone else do it this time?" If no one volunteers, you may need to assign roles.

If you do a regular rotation, it's helpful to clarify who is doing what ahead of time. You can communicate the role assignments to the team along with the agenda.

I've also seen teams select roles randomly. They use dice and each number represents a role. Playing cards or "pick a number between one and five" also work. Make it fun in any way you like, as long as assignments are arbitrary and fair.

It's very common for roles to become habitual. Cary always takes notes and Josh always keeps time. It's just how we do it. This is perfectly fine, as long as everyone is comfortable with their role and doesn't feel inhibited in their participation. Even if this is the case, you may still want to rotate roles on occasion for the reasons mentioned earlier.

No matter how you choose to assign them, make sure each person knows what role and responsibility she has at the start of the meeting. This ensures everyone is ready to take on whatever task is expected of them.

CHAPTER TEN REVIEW

- Clearly defined meeting roles can make any meeting run more smoothly.
- Examples of roles include meeting leader, facilitator, note-taker, timekeeper, and technology keeper.
- The leader is responsible for calling the meeting, setting the agenda, and ensuring proper preparation.
- The facilitator guides the group through the agenda, keeps everyone engaged and the conversation on track, and makes sure the norms are employed, with the purpose of moving the team toward a common goal.
- The note-taker keeps decisions and actions clear, records outcomes, and advances the conversation.
- The timekeeper alerts the group when it's exceeding allotted time for each subject, thereby helping to keep everyone on track and focused.
- The technology keeper makes sure all required tech elements are in place so they don't distract from the content of the meeting.
- You can assign roles based on talents and preferences, or at random to give everyone a chance to experience each. Rotating roles encourages skill building and ownership.
- Everyone in the meeting can be considered a participant, and it's important to prepare for that role as well.

CHAPTER TEN ACTION LIST

- Reflect on what formal or informal roles you usually play in meetings.
  - When you're a meeting leader, do you try to juggle all the meeting responsibilities yourself? Is it effective? How do you feel?
  - When you're a meeting participant, what are your responsibilities? How are you contributing to the success of the meeting? Are there ways you can support the meeting leader formally or informally?
- Ask yourself, what meeting roles and responsibilities can be helpful for your meetings to run effectively? How might you introduce the concept of roles into your meetings?
- Identify what roles you can start rotating in your meetings.
- If you already have roles, experiment with assigning them in a new way.

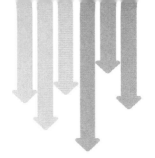

Chapter Eleven

Engagement

Engaging meeting participants does not only happen during the meeting. Remember, meetings are a cycle, not an event. Engagement happens before, during, and after: when you're planning the meeting, facilitating the conversation, and managing follow-through.

Many of the previous chapters covered how to engage participants before the meeting. Communicating with the participants prior to the meeting helps them realize why their participation is essential to its success. When you share the desired outcomes and agenda with them, you're painting a picture of what you'll achieve together as a team. As they read through the prework, they not only prepare themselves, but also intuit the thoughtfulness you've put into the meeting. Hopefully, you've built some excitement before they step into the meeting room.

Once the meeting itself begins, your job is to keep up the energy and engage the participants throughout your time together to bring out the best thinking in the most enjoyable way. You want to make the most of your time together so everyone walks away feeling good about what you've accomplished, as well as how you got there.

Engagement doesn't stop when the meeting ends. As meeting leader, you're responsible for maintaining the momentum to ensure follow-through. You need to continue to engage meeting participants, as well as other key stakeholders who need to be informed.

I explain many components of pre-meeting engagement in Chapters Six through Ten, so in this chapter, we'll focus on activities and techniques you can apply during and after the meeting.

ENGAGE PARTICIPANTS WITH A CHECK-IN

The moment you officially begin the meeting is your first opportunity to meaningfully engage the participants and set the tone for your remaining time together. The first few minutes should be used to help participants get into the mindset of the meeting. In many work environments, people are running from meeting to meeting and working until the last second on some task, possibly leaving it unfinished in order to pause for the meeting. With so much going on inside our heads, we need a period of transition. That's why I always recommend starting a meeting with an initial check-in. It's a way to help each team member put aside any distractions and help you, as the leader, get a feel for the room.

A check-in is also the ideal time to invite everyone's voice into the room, while acknowledging every person as being present and important to the coming conversation. If you speak at the beginning of the meeting, even if it's just to share what's on your mind, it makes it easier to speak up again later. The first time is always the hardest, so getting it out of the way up front will help make participants more comfortable and likely to engage later.

There are a variety of approaches to checking in. The traditional approach is to create space for people to unload what is on their mind taking up mental energy. Perhaps you're not feeling 100 percent and your mind is a bit foggy. Maybe you have a deadline looming and you're feeling the stress of it. Or maybe you're really excited about the vacation you're leaving for tomorrow. Anything occupying your brain can distract you from fully engaging in the meeting. Just mentioning it will help you put it aside and inform others of your current state.

A check-in of this style can be framed with a question such as:

- What's on your mind that you want to let go of?
- Anything you want to share with the group before we get into the meeting?
- How are you doing today?

With this framing, it's important to be clear this is not the time to jump into meeting content. Some people might use their check-in to say, "I was really excited by the prework I read, and this particular thing...," and it's easy to suddenly let the conversation spin out. Someone else will jump in to share their thoughts as well, and suddenly, you've skipped the first half of the agenda.

Let people know there will be time for that later, but for now, this time is reserved for connecting with each other and preparing for a rich conversation. It's perfectly fine to share your excitement for the meeting. In fact, it's wonderful when someone says, "I'm excited to be here and ready to dig in."

Also, let people know that if they feel ready to get this meeting going, and there's nothing they want to share, they can just say,

"I'm in." By doing so, they've acknowledged they had a chance to speak and confirmed they're ready to engage.

This type of check-in might seem like it's inviting people to take up a lot of time, but when conducted properly, it shouldn't. A skilled facilitator shared with me this trick: frame the time limit as a fun activity. "Let's challenge ourselves to keep our comments within 30 seconds. I'm going to set a timer and let's see if we can go 6-for-6 and all finish our remarks before it beeps." When you post the time limit for the check-in as a challenge, people often feel more excited than constrained.

Another type of check-in measures emotional readiness. One organization I know of starts every meeting by asking participants to rate their day on a scale of 1 to 10, 1 being the worst day of their lives and 10 being the best. If everybody in the group is below a 6, they don't even bother discussing the meeting content. If everybody's feeling stressed and pressured by something else, they reschedule the meeting so people can focus on what's bothering them or use some of the time to provide emotional support or do problem solving. The leader of this group knows if his people are not feeling good, he's not going to get the best out of them in the meeting. He chooses not to waste everyone's time with a meeting they're not mentally or emotionally prepared for.

A third type of check-in focuses on relationship building. Check-in is, after all, a time to see the people in the room as human beings, not just your colleagues. It's both a chance to get everybody talking and a chance to get to know people as their full selves. By using a fun question, you get to know a different side of your colleagues, while also creating a positive mood. There are random question generators online or you can make up your own. Several are available at www.meeteor.com/momentum/resources. A few I've used are:

- What was your favorite movie as a kid?
- If you could meet any historical figure, who would it be?
- What is your spirit vegetable and why?
- What is one fun thing you did this past weekend?

These questions are low pressure so everyone can contribute.

GIVE IT TIME ON THE AGENDA

Be sure you schedule time for the check-in on your agenda. Listing check-in as its own agenda topic makes it an official part of the agenda. If you don't, you risk not accounting for the time you'll need for it when planning, or forgetting about it in the moment.

To help estimate how much time you'll realistically need to devote to the check-in, consider the number of participants and the style of check-in you plan to use. Some check-ins require 15 seconds per person, while others need a full minute or 2. You're always better overestimating than underestimating. One of the worst situations in any meeting occurs when you've planned to take 5 minutes to do something and take 15, instead. This throws off the entire agenda and can inhibit the group from achieving the desired outcome.

BE A ROLE MODEL

In some cultures, starting a meeting with a check-in can be seen as touchy-feely or as a waste of time. Don't expect everyone on your team to embrace this practice on the first try. If checking in is unfamiliar in your organization, you can set the tone by modeling the desired behavior. If you're the meeting leader, introduce the process by sharing what's on your mind. If you think there is someone else on the team who will champion the importance of the check-in, consider asking him to start things off by sharing what's on his mind. This sets the tone and indicates to the rest of the group what is expected.

Generally, check-ins are a time for sharing, not responding. Demonstrate this behavior as well to remind people to listen and hold any comments. This can be challenging to do and isn't a hard and fast rule. Responding is a form of engagement in itself, which can be positive or negative. You want to avoid focusing on one person's remarks or turning the check-in into a conversation. You may need to be extra diligent in reminding yourself and others not to respond as people learn to be patient and get comfortable with the new process.

Role modeling is especially important if you want your team to talk about more personal matters. If people are used to coming to meetings and getting right to work, the idea of starting things off by chatting about their lives might make them uncomfortable. In a recent meeting, I used my check-in time to tell the group about my family's trip to Disney World. People responded briefly with, "That's so cool! I loved going to Disney when I was little." My one comment sparked a new connection. It opened the door for others to share more personal, familial check-ins, and we started our meeting on a positive note.

Check-in also gives you the chance to admit when you aren't in your best space. Maybe you just got back on a redeye and want to acknowledge that you're present, but no one should expect to get your best thinking. Maybe your child is sick and you need to have your phone out for the duration of the meeting in case the babysitter calls. Telling people about your circumstances up front absolves you from looking rude and lets them know they might not be getting your full focus.

SILENCE CAN HELP YOU BE PRESENT TOO

An alternative or addition to a verbal check-in is a moment of quiet. Some teams use 30 seconds or 1 minute of silence to set the tone before jumping into the agenda topics. When you're always in a rush, it's easy to bring the intensity and emotion with you. As a meeting leader, you may also struggle with getting participants' attention when it's time to actually start. People may have entered the room over the course of a few minutes and, instead of chit-chatting, they sat down and stared at their devices, checking email or otherwise distracting themselves. This can make it hard for you to get their attention and difficult for them to switch their focus. You'll be surprised by the power of 30 seconds of silence in which all devices are put away. Consider asking everyone to close their eyes and listen to their inner voice. Guide them to observe what's on their mind, acknowledge those thoughts, and put them aside. It's like a mini mindfulness moment and can become a beautiful ritual reminder for your team to live in the moment.

No matter how you conduct your meeting check-in, the goal is to help everyone be present and shift their focus to the meeting. As Suchman and Williamson put it in their 2007 paper "Principles and Practices of Relationship-Centered Meetings," the check-in step is "an investment in relationship building with the potential to pay large dividends in efficiency and performance."

CREATE PROPER CLOSURE WITH A CHECK-OUT

How you start the meeting is critical to engagement, and how you end is just as important. The check-out is similar to check-in, in that it's a time to assess where everyone is mentally. The goal is twofold: first, to make sure people don't walk out of the room feeling unsettled, wanting to say something but never feeling like they had the chance; and second, to reflect on the meeting and learn for the future.

The check-out process is often overlooked because people run out of time, the meeting gets derailed, or the advantages of an effective check-out are simply not understood. However, the potential risks of not having a proper meeting check-out are significant. Without effective and consistent check-outs, you run the risk of participants walking away confused, frustrated, or with unresolved questions, unaddressed needs, and unspoken ideas. Any of these could have negative effects, such as participants being unsure of what to do next, complaining to their colleagues, having negative emotions toward the team, or general disengagement. A little time invested in your check-out will go a long way.

CHECK-OUT TO GET THOUGHTS IN THE ROOM

No one benefits when people leave the meeting with unspoken thoughts. You can use the check-out to ensure everyone has a chance to clear their minds and put thoughts on the table. The meeting leader has gathered this group for this meeting because she believes each participant has an important opinion and perspective. This is the last chance to get it. In this way, check-out can be powerful in creating a positive team culture in which everyone's voice is appreciated.

A check-out negates the excuse of not having an opportunity to speak. One meeting I attended had a powerful turn during the check-out. A person who hadn't spoken much during the meeting shared a critical perspective saying, "I didn't have a chance to jump in earlier. The meeting was moving so quickly that by the time I thought of this, we were already past that point. But I think it's worth saying now." What she shared then changed the course of the meeting, prompting us to have a follow-up session and hold off making the decision, given this crucial insight.

This practice also helps curb hallway talk after a meeting, which is usually negative and counterproductive. The point of attending a meeting is to contribute your thoughts. If you don't agree with something or you feel like there's a point that went unsaid or unnoticed, speak up while the group is still gathered. If, instead, you harbor negative feelings and share them later in side conversations, you're contributing to an unhealthy team culture. A check-out is the ideal opportunity to say it now, not later.

To facilitate a check-out, use a framing question for participants to respond to. A few are listed here and more can be found in the Resources section of this book and at www.meeteor.com/momentum/resources. You can do it round-robin or popcorn style and ask the group,

- What else do you want to say before we totally wrap up?
- Any lingering thoughts or anything else you haven't yet shared?
- What's still on your mind that feels unsettled or unresolved?
- Any final thoughts?

These questions open the door for participants to share whatever it is that is still on their minds.

CHECK-OUT TO ASSESS THE MEETING

Another form of check-out is one in which participants reflect on the meeting. Ask people to identify what went well and supported the group to accomplish your desired outcome and what could be improved at a future meeting. Encourage participants to consider the structure of the agenda, any norms that were present or absent, and any facilitation techniques that were used or could have been. Generally, you'll want to steer away from individual behavior, especially if it was disruptive (how to address disruptive behaviors is mentioned later in this chapter).

To promote broad and reflective thinking, ask questions for people to respond to directly or use a sticky note activity to get people's thoughts quickly on paper. Here are a few questions:

- How did the meeting go? What worked that we should do again?
- What can we do better next time?
- What should we stop doing in our meetings?
- What ideas do you have for things we could try doing next time?

The framework of "start, stop, continue" is helpful for identifying practices that support an effective meeting.

PUT CHECK-OUT ON THE AGENDA TOO

Some teams separate the wrap-up process from the check-out. They use the wrap-up time to capture key takeaways and next steps (see more in Chapter Twelve), and the check-out time to invite final thoughts and feedback on the meeting process. No matter how you structure it, don't forget to include a check-out and/or wrap-up on your agenda. As with a check-in, you'll need to allocate time and want the visual reminder during the meeting to end the discussion with it. Otherwise, you may run out of time. It's easy to get excited about the conversation, run over time, and be forced to end with no real sense of closure. Make sure everyone on the team recognizes the value of a check-out and wrap-up, and be sure to allow appropriate time for either or both.

DESIGN MEETING ACTIVITIES FOR ENGAGEMENT

The design, or structure, of the meeting greatly contributes to how it unfolds. When planning the design, think about the flow of topics and activities that will make the conversation most productive and keep the energy up.

The flow of topics is often intuitive. Align on the issue before generating ideas. Clarify options before making a decision. What is often overlooked, though, is the way energy or engagement flows during these phases of the conversation. When you design your meeting with how people will participate in addition to what they will discuss, you'll reach a new level of contribution where quieter people share more, louder people make space, more ideas are generated, and less unproductive conflict arises.

Which activities you choose will depend on the type of meeting you have, the number of people in attendance, and the topics you need to cover. You might include some high-energy activities to get people moving. You might use some low-energy options to give people quiet time to mull something over. If the group is big, you might want to break into groups to give everyone time to speak. No matter the reason for using activities, it's important to think about how they fit into each phase of the agenda and contribute to the overall experience.

The following are just a few examples of activities you can consider when you design your meeting activities. You don't necessarily need to include these activities on the agenda you share with the participants, but do keep your own personal notes or micro-agenda that details how you'll run the activities.

BREAK IT UP

Get people talking by breaking them into small groups. If you have more than 6 people in a meeting, sitting in one big conversation for an hour or more can feel like an energy drain. Sometimes time constraints make it hard to get through a full agenda with everyone verbally participating in the conversation. If you break people into pairs, triads, or quads, you can get more conversation going. This actively engages more people and results in more thinking being shared.

Depending on what you need to cover, each small group can discuss the same or different issues. You can assign each team a topic, let them discuss it, and ask them to report back to the group. You can divide people into groups based on what topic is most interesting or relevant to them or do it randomly. This divide-and-conquer approach is especially helpful for large meetings of 12 or more people, as well as brainstorming sessions.

After the allotted time in small groups, ask a member of each to report on the highlights or takeaways of their conversation. Alternatively, have them write on a board or flip chart and then walk around the room to see what other groups wrote. This technique is called "Gallery Walk." The groups can then converse about what they saw or write directly on the other groups' boards by adding additional thoughts or starring things they agree with. Getting people to physically move stimulates energy while supporting a productive meeting.

You might be surprised, but this small group approach works for virtual meetings too. I participated in a 90-minute video conference call with almost 20 people where we broke into pairs for the check-in. The meeting leader sent an email prior to the start of the meeting listing who would call whom at what number. When the meeting started, we had to do a quick rearrangement due to some tardy participants. The leader instructed us to call our assigned partner and set a timer on our phones for 6 minutes. Each person had 3 minutes to share and, when the timer went off, it was time to rejoin the main conference line. To be honest, I was skeptical at first. Would people take this seriously? Would they return to the main conversation on time? To my delight, as far as I could tell, it worked beautifully. I had a lovely conversation with my partner. We rejoined the group and within 30 seconds, everyone was back on the line. We ended the check-in with a quick sharing. The leader asked for 3 people to share a highlight from their conversation, which helped us all connect more broadly and was a nice transition into the rest of the meeting.

STICKY NOTES OR WRITE IT DOWN

Not all time in a meeting needs to be spent talking. Introverts especially appreciate having quiet time to reflect and think before jumping into the discussion. Sticky notes are a fantastic tool for gathering thoughts from many people all at once. Lay out a framework and ask people to write one idea per sticky note. The framing could be any of the following:

- A brainstorming session, e.g. how might we increase engagement with our followers on social media?
- A feedback request, e.g. what aspects of our collaboration worked/didn't work for our latest product launch?
- A question generator, e.g. what questions should we be asking to determine whether this decision is a good one?

If you're not all in the same room, use an online tool such as a shared Google Doc or Trello board to allow everyone to contribute ideas. Give people a few minutes of quiet time to think and write first. I often set a timer for 2 minutes and then ask the group if they want more time. When the writing phase is finished, people can either go round-robin and share one idea at a time or post their sticky notes on the wall (physical or virtual) in clusters. If you go the second route, give everyone a few minutes to read over each other's ideas before diving into a conversation.

This is one of my favorite techniques for engaging people. I even use it when there're only 2 or 3 of us, because it really gets your brain juices flowing and generates lots of content in a short amount of time. It also enables you to quickly see where there is alignment by clustering similar ideas.

Don't forget to take photos of any content generated on flip charts and sticky notes. These photos should become part of the meeting record. There is great content in them you don't want to lose. No need to type up the information unless you want it searchable or more legible. Just paste the photos into the meeting notes or store them in the appropriate file and attach them to the email sent with the notes.

RESPECT EVERYONE'S TIME—AND MAKE SURE EVERYONE ELSE DOES THE SAME

Starting and ending on time is the most important way you can respect people's time. There is no problem with ending early, but try to avoid ending late. When you run over, you may have people trickling out as they run to other meetings. Now you've lost the opportunity for closure and clarity of next steps. If it looks like you're going to run out of time, acknowledge it and ask the group if they can stay an extra 10 or so minutes. This way, even if no one rushes out the door, people will be less likely to secretly peek at their watch while feeling the meeting is aimlessly dragging on and on.

It's important to create a culture where being late to a meeting is unacceptable, but leaders should also be willing to examine reasons for lateness, especially if it's a recurring problem. There are typically three reasons why people are late to meetings:

- They physically can't get there on time.
- They are not managing their time well.
- Something interrupts or delays them.

Each of these needs to be addressed and solved. In the first scenario, there are legitimate limitations to how quickly we can move. It's unreasonable to expect someone who is in a meeting that ends at 3:30 p.m. to instantly appear at your meeting that starts at the same time. In some companies, meetings are always scheduled for 25- or 55-minute increments, attempting to leave transition time. Unfortunately, it's a lot of extra work to make your calendar system work this way, given most default to 30 or 60 minutes. Regardless, people need time to walk across the building, use the restroom, or find the dial in, and then wait for the lovely lady's voice to say, "If you're the meeting leader, press pound now."

Assume your meetings will always start 2–3 minutes after the scheduled start time. If participants are more than 5 minutes late, it may be time to intervene. I never recommend pointing out lateness to the whole group and trying to shame someone into a timely arrival. Instead, start by having a private conversation with the offender, during which you try to understand the cause of their delay. Once you've unearthed the reason, try to work together to resolve the problem.

For example, I know someone whose company holds a meeting every Tuesday at 8:00 a.m. She is always late because she has to drop her kids off at school at 7:30 and it's a 40-minute commute from there to the office. Their office policy is that the workday officially starts at 8:30 a.m., but of course, people work earlier or later as needed. After a few weeks of trying to get there on time and failing, she articulated this conflict to her team leader. Unfortunately, even after raising the problem several times, her manager ignored her complaint, and she continued to be late. In this case, her team leader was not displaying good leadership qualities. Instead of turning a blind eye, they should experiment with finding a solution that works for everyone. Maybe this woman could call in from her car while she's in transit if the meeting time can't be changed. Perhaps the meeting could be pushed back 15 minutes to accommodate her schedule. Maybe there is another day of the week where 8:00 a.m. works because her partner can take the kids to school. There needs to be an openness and willingness to compromise from both parties.

The second cause of tardiness, poor time management, needs to be addressed as a professional development goal. Time management skills are essential to success in the modern business world. No one should be chronically late because they can't seem to stop other work to transition to the meeting. Luckily, a few simple tricks can help with this problem, although it may be a deeper issue that needs further attention.

Try doing these things for yourself and suggesting them to anyone who needs a little extra reminder to wrap up work and head to a meeting:

- Use calendar reminders to your advantage. Figure out how much time you need to transition from whatever you're typically doing to a meeting. Set the default reminder on all calendar events to that time. If you need 3 minutes, don't set it for 5 or you'll end up ignoring it (or maybe you already do!) knowing you can sneak in another 2 minutes of work.
- Set a timer or alarm on your phone to alert you when it's time to wrap up.
- Put a sticky note on the corner of your computer screen with a note that you need to stop at a certain time. Even this simple visual reminder can make a difference.
- Turn off other alerts so when your phone buzzes, it's either a phone call, text message, or meeting reminder, none of which you should typically ignore altogether.

The last problem, unexpected delays, is the hardest. Usually this does not manifest as chronic lateness. On occasion, a prior meeting will run over or traffic will be terrible, a colleague will stop you in the hall with something urgent, or your kid's pediatrician will pick that exact moment to call you about a billing problem. If a person is occasionally late, don't overthink it.

USE NORMS TO ADDRESS LATENESS

Norms are a great tool for creating a shared understanding of how tardy participants will be treated. Each company must do what's best for its own specific circumstances, but I recommend establishing the understanding that if you're late, it's up to you to get on the same page as everyone else. Stopping the meeting to recap for latecomers not only leaves other participants feeling frustrated, it lets them know they too can be late because there is no consequence.

Some norms explicitly address the issue of catching latecomers up to speed. Others are a bit softer in their presentation. Consider these two variations on the same theme:

- We don't stop to catch anyone up. If you're late, you're late.
- If you're late, feather yourself in to avoid disrupting the conversation.

Both make it known that when you arrive after the meeting has started, no one is going to catch you up. It's your responsibility to figure out what you missed. If you need clarification on something you think has already come up, you can say, "I apologize for being late. I was curious about this one thing. If you've already discussed it, we don't need to go back." When you do this, you're gently asking for information you might have missed. You're not walking into the room and saying, "Sorry I'm late, guys! What'd I miss?"

If you're the meeting leader, you can acknowledge a latecomer by saying, "Jim, I'm glad you could join us. We just finished talking about this topic and made this decision and now we're here on the agenda." It's brief, but it gets the person up to speed on the key information they need to know. If you go this route, do it as lightly as possible, then move on.

If the latecomer is a leader of the organization or another more senior person, it's hard, if not impossible, to say, "We're not catching you up." A great way to avoid lateness from higher-ups is to make sure your meeting is not scheduled immediately after another appointment. This isn't always possible, but most people schedule their days in half-hour or hour increments. If a person has one meeting from 9 to 9:30 and you schedule your meeting for 9:30, you're guaranteeing their late arrival. There is no harm in scheduling that same meeting for 9:40 to give them time to walk from one end of the building to another and account for the prior meeting running a few minutes over.

If the late person is a critical decision maker, it might be worth waiting for her before starting. Use the time with the people who are present to do more checking in, bonding, and relationship building. You also can give people permission to stay on their devices until the latecomer arrives. If you've checked in with that person's assistant and she will be there in 10 minutes, let people keep working until the meeting officially starts.

Leaving early can be just as disruptive as arriving late. Be mindful of what happens when someone has to step out of a meeting before it's over. If you know you have to leave early, tell the other participants at the beginning during the check-in. Don't surprise everybody partway through the meeting. Beyond being disruptive, a surprise exit does not allow the facilitator to rearrange the agenda if certain items require your presence, nor can the group include you in decision making and task assignment that typically happens at the end of the meeting.

If it's appropriate, you can offer your final insights before leaving. You can say, "I just want to say two quick things, and I apologize, I have to get going. Here are the two things on my mind, and I look forward to hearing what the group decides." This gives the team the permission to move forward without you. It lets them know you trust them to decide in your absence and you plan to get informed afterward.

CREATE AN OPEN AND INCLUSIVE MEETING ENVIRONMENT

Ideally, everyone in the meeting feels welcome and openly shares their thoughts. Unfortunately, most meetings are far from the ideal. When people aren't comfortable, confident, or engaged in a meeting, the conversation suffers, diminishing the good work your meeting was intended to do. Sometimes this manifests as dead silence after you've asked for input. Participants hold back their thoughts, are unsure of what is appropriate, are hesitant to speak first, or are distracted and aren't paying attention, so have lost track of the question asked. Sometimes people filter their opinions or censor their comments to conform with the group or leader. Other times, someone fights too hard for her ideas, acts defensively when challenged, and shuts down communication and healthy debate. While it's beyond frustrating to be in a meeting with any of these scenarios, the worst part is that people are often having the "real" conversation after the meeting, in the hallway, or over lunch. All that good thinking is lost. What a waste.

People are hard-wired to act conservatively around authority. Business and management professors James R. Detert at the University of Virginia and Ethan R. Burris at the University of Texas at Austin conclude that "a fear of consequences (embarrassment, isolation, low performance ratings, lost promotions) and a sense of futility (the belief that saying something won't make a difference, so why bother?)" are the main inhibitors to candor at work.

Without an environment of open communication in your meetings, you can't bring out the best thinking of the group. Creating a culture in which people feel valued, respected, and willing to be vulnerable is no easy feat. It takes time to develop that kind of trust, and there are often outside contexts you may or may not be able to influence. Interpersonal dynamics, office politics, and personalities all play a role in shaping the culture and, depending on the size of your organization and your role, are typically beyond your control.

Despite the complexity, there are things you can do to move your team and your meetings in the right direction. Norms are a great starting point. There are a number of norms designed to help draw more honest voices into your conversation. For example, norms such as, "all ideas are good ideas," or, "half-baked ideas are welcome," can create room for different thinking. If someone has a thought that is not fully formed, rather than focusing on the fear of having an incomplete idea, they have, at least in theory, the freedom to put it before the group without judgment. Obviously, just having a norm doesn't automatically change behavior or people's deep emotions, but it's a signal that you want that kind of environment. To learn more about norms that engage meeting participants and how to use them during meetings, visit Chapter Nine.

HELP PEOPLE FEEL THEIR VOICES ARE VALUED

In her book *Presence: Bringing Your Boldest Self to Your Biggest Challenges*, Harvard Business School professor Amy Cuddy shares that one reason people struggle to engage in stressful situations such as meetings is due to their feelings of powerlessness. Psychologists call it the "imposter syndrome." People who experience it often feel like they don't deserve to be there, or discredit what they have to offer. If you notice some participants always seem hesitant to share their ideas or speak up in meetings, they may need a confidence boost to help them see you value their opinion. Consider approaching them before the meeting to reinforce that you've asked them to join the meeting for a reason.

I did this with a colleague once who always seemed to have brilliant additions to the conversation, but rarely spoke without being specifically called upon. I asked for 5 minutes with her the day before the meeting and said, "I want to check in with you about the meeting tomorrow. I really want you to speak up because I value what you have to say. I hope you'll be more proactive in sharing your thoughts." My goal was to help build her confidence to speak up and participate, which in fact it did. She wasn't suddenly the most talkative in the group, but I did notice her jumping in more than usual. After the meeting, I thanked her for her participation and the valuable ideas she contributed.

This approach also works well in specific situations, such as when you've invited a more junior person to a meeting with senior leadership. If you intend for this person to sit quietly and listen, let him know. If you intend for him to join in and contribute, let him know that too. By explicitly sharing your desire, you're giving him permission to speak up, even if he feels out of place. It also works well if you know certain people have strong opposing opinions from the rest of the group. If you alert them ahead of time that you specifically want them to share those thoughts, they'll be more comfortable voicing unpopular views.

RECOGNIZE THAT EXTROVERTS AND INTROVERTS ENGAGE IN DIFFERENT WAYS

While extroverts need external stimulation to do their best thinking, introverts tend to process things internally. Extroverts generally think out loud while engaging in a discussion; introverts often prefer to clarify their thoughts internally before speaking. Because of this, introverts can be mislabeled as shy or standoffish, when they actually do want to engage if given the right opportunity.

Different activities will appeal to introverts and extroverts. To help your introverted colleagues engage more deeply, try incorporating an activity that includes quiet time for solo thinking. You might suggest the groupthink about an issue for a few minutes, write down their ideas, then go around the table and share. This provides time for internal reflection and processing everyone can benefit from.

Many introverts prefer small group conversations to large ones. Breaking into pairs or trios is another way to help them feel more comfortable. You can also use your role as facilitator to draw introverts out. You just need to be conscious of who is speaking and who isn't. You might use a norm to set expectations for everyone to participate, such as, "Everyone in this meeting is here for a reason, so speak up." Then reference this norm when you want the quieter folk to chime in.

As the meeting facilitator, pay attention to who has been silent. Create a space for them to speak by saying, "We've heard a lot from some of our folks, but I'd like to hear from those we haven't heard from yet. For those of you who haven't spoken yet, what do you want to share? What have you been thinking about?" Additionally, as you're transitioning from one topic to another, you can make space for everyone to contribute without cutting anyone off by asking quieter people to speak first. You might say, "For this next subject, I'd like to have people who haven't spoken yet start us off."

As mentioned earlier, if you anticipate someone will be a quieter participant at the meeting, approach him beforehand to tell him why you invited him and what items you're specifically looking forward to hearing his thoughts on. This lets him know you want him to speak up, and you'll likely call on him in the meeting if he doesn't. It can be jarring to have the group leader call you out by name, and say, "Rob, we haven't heard from you. What are you thinking?" If you're not prepared, it can evoke flashbacks of the teacher calling on you in school when you have no idea what the answer is. It's not a good feeling and may be interpreted that you want him to look foolish in front of your colleagues. Having a heads up can help the quieter people feel ready to engage when asked.

BALANCE PARTICIPATION

We've all been to a meeting where someone dominated the conversation. They took over the stage as if they couldn't stop talking. They seemed to have an opinion about every topic, were the first to jump in, and took valuable airtime from others.

SOME PEOPLE SHOULD SPEAK LESS

If you already know who those potential "dominators" are, you can check in with them beforehand and delicately ask them to make room for others. The way you frame it depends on the person and how self-aware they are. Some people are very aware they talk a lot, while others don't recognize such behavior in themselves.

I had this difficult conversation once. I sat down with a colleague more senior than I was and explained, "I'm not sure you're aware you do this, but you often get going on a topic and it's hard to cut you off or reel you in. You always have interesting things to say, but it's not always productive in our meetings. Would you be okay if I cut you off to keep us on track?" He was a bit surprised and a little taken aback, but ultimately agreed. It was still difficult for me to jump in while he was talking in a meeting, but I had more confidence he wouldn't respond negatively when I did so. What I didn't expect was for him to be more self-aware and able to control himself mid-thought. I noticed after our little talk that, occasionally, he'd get going and then say, "Actually, I think I've gone a little off-topic. Where were we on the agenda?" Sometimes, people just need to be aware of their own behavior and its effect on others.

Depending on the person and your relationship with them, you might be able to simply say, "I really value your contribution and that's why you're invited to this meeting, but I want to make sure we have time and space for some of our other participants.

I'd like for you to try and contain some of your thinking, and I'd be happy to meet with you after the meeting to discuss anything you feel you didn't get to express during the conversation." It's straightforward and offers an alternative way to share thinking so the person doesn't feel his contributions are unwanted.

You also can have a norm about balancing participation. Norms such as "step forward and step back" and "make room for all voices" set the expectation that at some point in the meeting, the chattiest among the group should take a break to let the quieter members chime in. As the meeting leader or facilitator, you can say, "Before anyone responds, I hope you'll step forward or back if you haven't yet," or, "I want to pause for a moment and see if you all think we've made space for all voices." Calling on these norms during the meeting helps people check their own behavior, encouraging them to become more self-aware.

SOME PEOPLE SHOULD SPEAK LAST

In many cultures and organizations, whatever the leader says goes—whether it's intentional or not. People don't feel comfortable offering alternative ideas or opinions once a leader states her position, so the conversation shuts down. The acronym "HiPPO" says it all—the "highest paid person's opinion" is what matters. In these circumstances, consider asking the leaders present in the meeting to speak last. By having the leader speak last, you're creating an opportunity for the rest of the participants to speak more honestly and even influence what the leader ultimately says. As you do this, be conscious of not developing a habit where the leader always gets the last word; this is just another form of the leader shutting down conversation. Aim to let conversation unfold unfettered, then have the leader contribute, and end with additional conversation.

This can be challenging for some leaders, especially if they are used to speaking freely. Your job is to help them understand that by holding back, they're avoiding groupthink and allowing everyone else to put forth their best thinking. People can and should be allowed to speak after, and even argue with, the leader, but it takes trust and a specific culture for this to happen. Asking leaders to speak last is a first step to building a culture in which all perspectives are really welcomed and seniority does not mean smarter.

The purpose of having a leader speak after others is to encourage all opinions be put on the table, which is in itself not always easy. As people become more comfortable with speaking their minds, you can transition from leaders speaking last to leaders engaging in conversation like everyone else. By this point, hopefully people are more comfortable with leaders present in the room so rich debate can ensue.

RE-ENGAGE THE DISENGAGED

I'm sure you've been in a meeting where you've noticed one or more of these behaviors:

- Participants are periodically checking their phones, tablets, or other devices.
- People appear busy with other work, distracted, and absent-minded.
- When you ask for someone's opinion, they seem startled and ask you to repeat the question.
- People repeat questions or comments as if they are new ideas, not realizing those points were already made or discussed.

Honestly, I've been in plenty of meetings where I'm the one doing those bad behaviors. In these situations, to everyone else at the meeting, it appears you are physically in the room—or online if it's a virtual meeting—but it seems as if they've lost you.

As you likely know from your own experience, people disengage from meetings for many reasons. While it's easy to point fingers and assume they just don't care or don't respect those in the meeting, it's not always that simple. Sometimes you might not feel like you are part of the conversation, or that you can contribute to the discussion. This is especially true when you've joined a meeting virtually but a number of other people are co-located. You might feel your presence at this meeting is unnecessary, whether that be true or not. Or, you may have other things going on that are keeping you from giving the meeting your full attention.

Regardless of why someone disengages from a conversation, it's your responsibility as a meeting leader to re-engage them. You can use eye contact or a long pause to help them recognize their behavior and adjust accordingly. You can also call on norms the team has set by saying, "Hey guys, we agreed to no checking emails in this meeting." Or, consider having an off-line conversation to learn the cause of their behavior and share feedback.

If you decide to have a separate conversation, start by listening. You can say something like, "Sammy, I noticed that we lost your attention for a while during the meeting earlier. I'm curious what was going on that made you check out." When you uncover the underlying reasons, you'll be able to take actions to address the issue. Maybe you discover he is really stressed about another priority or that he didn't feel he had anything to add and thought he shouldn't have been in the meeting in the first place.

Or, maybe he won't have any good reason and will see that his behavior, which he thought no one noticed, was very noticeable. In any case, you should still share your feedback about how this made you feel and in what ways you believe it affected the group and meeting outcomes. End the conversation by problem solving. Say, "Next time you've got a lot going on, tell me. Maybe we can figure out another way for you to contribute so you don't need to be in the meeting." Or, "Sammy, I'm sorry it was unclear why I asked you to participate. What I'm hoping you'll add is..." Or, "I hope you'll give the meeting your full attention in the future. I'm open to suggestions for how to make the meeting more engaging and interesting if you have any." Creating an engaging meeting is both the meeting leader and participants' responsibility.

However you address it, just make sure you do. Don't ignore the disengaged behavior, because it impacts the entire group's dynamics, even when no one voices the concern. If you allow this behavior in your meetings, you are complicit and only adding to others' frustration. This behavior can become toxic and hinder the group's ability to have an effective and enjoyable meeting.

Finally, if you are often the one disengaging, check in with yourself to understand why and take steps to address it. For example, close down other apps and hide your phone when you're on a video conference to reduce distractions. Or, reach out to the meeting leader to discuss your concern with him.

ENGAGE BY USING DIFFERENT VOTING METHODS

There are many ways to make voting productive, fun, and engaging. Sitting around in one large group saying, "Raise your hand if you like idea A. Okay, how about B?" is not only boring, it can make people uncomfortable or miss the nuanced opinions. It takes courage to be the only one who votes for B or goes against the boss's vote. It may also be hard to vote for A or B if you're not fully convinced of either. Instead, try one of these voting activities:

DOT VOTES

Give each meeting participant three (or five or one) "dots" with which to vote. Dots can be stickers, sticky notes, or making a check mark or star with a pen or marker. Each person can decide to put all three by a single idea or spread them out among a few. It's up to them, and enables them to show not only preference but enthusiasm. Plus, it's much more fun than counting raised hands.

FIST OF 5

Ask participants to raise the number of fingers corresponding with their level of agreement with the decision. A closed fist is 100 percent against, whereas a full open hand displaying 5 fingers is 100 percent in agreement. Voters can raise any number of fingers that accurately represents their feelings. You can then focus the conversation on what reservations Mamie has that made her choose a 2, or move forward with the decision as long as no one is below a 3 (neutral), if that's what you've agreed to. This is especially great for virtual meetings when all participants are using video.

KEEP THE CONVERSATION MOVING

To achieve a meeting's desired outcome, you need to keep the conversation moving forward. This isn't always easy to do. The conversation can spin or go off on a tangent. People won't stop talking or won't let something go. When you find the conversation has gotten stuck or you need to move forward without stepping on toes, try one of the following approaches:

IDENTIFY WHAT'S HOLDING YOU BACK

You might be trying to make a decision or clarify next steps, but it seems like you aren't able to get there. Sometimes, that's because you're missing critical information. Sometimes, it's because you don't have the right person in the room. You can't always anticipate these things ahead of time. Even with the most thoughtful planning, these issues occasionally surface while you're in the meeting, and they make the conversation spin. When it drags on, people can easily feel annoyed and frustrated.

When you notice the conversation spinning but don't know exactly why, pose it to the group. Offer your observation by saying, "It seems like we've been talking about this idea and running in circles for the last few minutes. What's hindering us? What other things do we need to move forward?" This way, everyone is aware of the situation they're in, and finding a solution to the problem becomes everyone's responsibility. In the case of a decision, try taking a straw poll using Fist of 5. Then go around and have each person who is less than a 3 or 4, your choice, say why they're feeling low and what would need to happen to move them up.

If it's clear what's getting in the way, acknowledge the issue to the group by saying, "It seems like we're missing some critical information," or, "It seems like we can't really lock this down or resolve this issue without having so-and-so in the room, so why don't we pause this conversation and keep going with the agenda?"

There is no reason to continue down a path if you don't have what you need to bring it to resolution.

Sometimes, groups become stuck because members are risk-averse or fearful of commitment. I was once in a meeting where one of the participants wanted a piece of financial information before approving a decision. We started by asking if the information would fundamentally change his position. Surprisingly, when you ask people how the information will change their position, many realize it won't and are able to move on without it. He said, "If the information says A, then I'd be comfortable with this, but if it says B, then I would not." The next question was, "What are the chances the information's going to say B?" The answer was "very low." I suggested we decide based on the assumption B was not the case, and we were able to move forward with a tentative decision. One person was then assigned to gather the information and share it by email by the end of the week.

Had we not moved forward with a tentative decision, we would have had to delay the decision while someone gathered the information, then had another meeting in which the information was presented, and likely rehashed much of what we'd already discussed. With the contingent decision, we knew if the information came back as A, there was no need to do anything further. If, by chance, it came back as B, we could regroup and revisit the decision.

SAVE IT FOR LATER

When an off-topic idea comes up in a meeting, it can be interesting but not relevant or urgent. These threads of conversation don't help achieve the desired outcome, but can end up monopolizing a meeting where they don't belong. To bring your group back to the important topics at hand, try using a "back burner." Some teams also call it "parking lot" or "issue bin." Whatever you call it, the function is to capture off-agenda items to be saved for another time. Meeteor has a standing norm to use a back burner. Anyone can say in any meeting, "This seems like a back-burner topic," and we'll write it in the notes and move on.

If you can, create a physical storage place, such as a whiteboard or shared document on screen, where you list items to be followed up on later. This helps people feel heard rather than shut down. Their ideas are recorded and won't be forgotten. It also keeps people from withholding good ideas not entirely in line with the current conversation. When used like this, putting something on the back burner is a way to avoid losing or ignoring ideas so you can figure out what to do with them later. It lets participants share random thoughts without throwing the whole conversation off. Be sure to transfer back-burner items to the meeting notes so they can be revisited, if necessary.

The clearer your agenda is, the more aligned people will be on what items go into the back burner. Over time, you may find people actively calling on the back burner: "I know it's not relevant right now, but I have a thought for the back burner. I'd like more information on..." Or, "Maybe this is a 'bike rack' topic, but what do you think about X?" A back burner, parking lot, issue bin, bike rack, tabling it—these are all acceptable ways to recognize the energy around an idea but hold it for later.

If time permits at the end of the meeting, you can quickly review back-burner items. Sometimes, the back burner is just to hold ideas and, as the conversation evolves, the problem or idea might resolve itself so there is no need to follow up. Other times, it's an item requiring action or more conversation. In these cases, assign the item an owner who will take the appropriate next step.

ASK POWERFUL QUESTIONS

Asking questions can help you bring out the best of your colleagues and move the conversation forward. What I love about questions is that anyone can ask them. Here are some common questions you can use:

Would You Say More about That?

This is one of the most powerful questions I use to draw out ideas from others. Sometimes, when you hear a comment from a colleague, you're not 100 percent sure about why she proposed the idea or what the rationale is for her suggestion. Instead of reacting to or judging the comment, pause and ask, "Would you say more about it?"

I find this question powerful, because you don't need to know anything or express any judgment when asking it. It immediately helps people open up and provide more information. It demonstrates curiosity on your part and surfaces perspectives that would otherwise go unspoken.

This question saved me from making a terrible decision at one meeting. A participant, Megan, was sharing that she'd like to bring in a speaker for one of our upcoming board meetings. A few weeks prior, I had introduced Megan to this speaker, so I was glad she had found their conversation useful enough to want to bring the speaker to the whole group. Out of sheer curiosity, I said, "Megan, tell me more about your conversation with Jenna and what she will likely talk about with us." Thank goodness I'd said something! We were all about to go on Megan's recommendation, but Megan's response turned us around completely: "Oh, I haven't actually spoken with her. I thought you wanted me to bring her in and the conversation was a formality. Is that not the case?" I had only just met Jenna at a networking event and thought she might be interesting. I had no intention of bringing her in "just because." As it was Megan's domain, I'd figured they could talk and Megan could decide if it was the right fit. Apparently, that didn't come across clearly in my email. The simple phrase "tell me more" surfaced assumptions on both our parts.

Why?

Originally developed by Sakichi Toyoda and used at Toyota, "5 Whys" is a questioning technique to explore the root cause of a problem or uncover the underlying assumption of a statement. Most of us are accustomed to asking why only once, if at all. Toyoda points out that asking why five times will illuminate deeper thinking. How many whys you ask is up to you. For example, when someone shares a statement, "I think we should run a weekly meeting on this project," you can ask, "Why do you think we should run weekly meetings?" He might reply, "I think weekly meetings help us to stay aligned as a team." You can either stop there and discuss whether a weekly meeting is the optimal way to stay aligned or continue asking why. For example, when you ask another "why," he might say, "I think weekly meetings are the only way to hold people accountable." Again, you can discuss or ask why. This process can go on until you've reached a point of clarity, understanding, or alignment.

Anything to Add?

When you're in a divergent conversation in which people are sharing opinions, generating ideas, or essentially not driving to a decision or a next step, you can move things forward by asking if anyone has anything new or pressing to add. Create a sense of urgency if there is limited time left for this topic, by saying, "We only have 2 minutes until we need to move on. Does anyone have anything new to add?" Help people censor themselves by being clear only burning issues should be discussed at this point. This should help people refrain from repeating something that's already been said.

Can We Move On?

It's no fun to be caught in a situation where it seems like the conversation isn't nearing resolution, yet you're running out of time. When a conversation is at risk of being left unfinished or taking over the agenda, ask the group if they'd like to extend the allotted time by a few minutes or put the topic aside for another time. Sometimes, you need to finish one conversation in order to keep going with the next. Other times, it's more appropriate to revisit a topic after the meeting or at a separate meeting. Either way, you're acknowledging the agenda and making a conscious decision to follow or dismiss it. If you do decide to keep going down the same path, agree on a time limit and check in again if the additional time still doesn't seem to be enough. At that point, you may also be missing something critical that is keeping you from reaching a resolution.

If We Do This, Then What?

If it seems like the group's energy is moving in one direction, acknowledge the consensus around the decision and ask for relevant concerns and next steps. Don't just keep talking about the merits of the idea. Sometimes, we get so excited about our ideas, we want to keep talking about them. Challenge the group to think of anything related to the decision that has not yet been said. What unintended consequences might occur? What resources will be needed? What exactly do we need to do to make this decision happen? At this point, you're ready to focus on two things: first, explore any possible downfalls, and, if there are none, the conversation can end; second, identify any action items and next steps.

There are various kinds of questions that can help you move the conversation forward. Check out our website at www.meeteor.com/momentum/resources to find more information on this topic.

ENGAGE, EVEN WHEN YOU DON'T ATTEND

If you need to attend a meeting but can't because you are sick, out of the office, or attending to a higher-priority matter, you are not necessarily free from responsibility. There are other ways to engage in a meeting without being present.

Get your voice in the room by sharing your thoughts ahead of time. If prework is sent, review it and send an email with your ideas and questions to the meeting leader or another participant who can represent your perspective in the meeting. Offer to leave comments on a document or provide input in another way. Alternatively, schedule a brief conversation with the team leader to learn more and share your ideas, and ask him to bring your thoughts to the meeting.

Make it clear you are willing to accept the outcomes of the meeting because the group needs to move forward. Tell the leader you are willing to take on appropriate tasks. This is a great way to show the team you are still invested, even if you can't be at the meeting.

After the meeting, stay informed by asking for the meeting notes and inquiring about any next steps requiring your attention. Sometimes you are assigned tasks in a meeting, but nobody tells you about them. Don't let that interfere with your engagement. I like to schedule a reminder for myself to follow up after the meeting to inquire about any outcomes that may affect my work.

On the flip side, you can decline meetings where your real-time input is unnecessary. By asking the meeting organizer whether your participation is critical, you raise awareness that you are okay with not being invited to meetings. Go one step further by offering to provide input in other ways, such as those mentioned above.

PARTICIPANTS AFTER THE MEETING

The meeting doesn't end when you hang up the phone or walk out the door. Who you engage with and how will depend on the specifics of your meeting, but, essentially, your job is to support follow-through and inform key stakeholders so all your good work gets put into motion.

ENSURE PROPER FOLLOW-THROUGH

It's helpful to understand why follow-through is such a challenge.

One typical reason is the meeting outcomes aren't clear. Most conversations generate multiple ideas for next steps, but it's not always obvious which of them the team intends to take. If someone says, "We should get those numbers from Bill," more information is needed to effectively execute that task. Is this an actual next step or a proposed next step that is really a "nice to have" and doesn't need to be done? What exact numbers are needed? Who is going to get them from Bill? Once they are obtained, what does the group intend to do with them? Eliminate ambiguity so everyone knows exactly what to do. For help on how to clarify next steps, see Chapter Twelve: Notes.

A related problem could be an unclear timeline. If you have all the answers to the questions above but no idea when those numbers are to be produced by, it's possible the task will either be forgotten or pushed to the bottom of the to-do pile. I may not be intentionally avoiding a task, but if I'm balancing multiple projects and dozens of to-dos, anything without a deadline automatically ends up lowest on my list. Assign a specific due date, even an arbitrary one, for any task identified in a meeting. This helps people prioritize accordingly and drives action.

Another problem is lack of accountability. If the numbers from Bill are due by the next meeting, but you know no one is going to ask whether they were obtained, there is no incentive to do the task. No consequence means no motivation. Again, people generally aren't trying to derail the work or deviously avoiding responsibilities, they're simply too busy with other work they'll be held accountable for. Too many next steps go undone without any consequence, perpetuating the idea that meeting tasks aren't integral to a project's success. This is why it's in everyone's best interest to only assign next steps that must get done, and then make sure they do.

If you've done the work of clearly identifying next steps and assigning them owners and due dates, you're ready to support follow-through.

CHECK IN ON THE STATUS OF PRIOR MEETING OUTCOMES

As a meeting leader, you can build accountability for meeting tasks into your regular workflow. Encourage team members to transfer their assignments into their regular task system. If you use a collaborative task system, you can either add the meeting tasks for them or even type them into the task system during your wrap-up at the end of the meeting. You want to build an atmosphere where meeting tasks are taken as seriously as any other task.

Some teams have a practice of reviewing the status of open tasks from previous meetings during the following meeting. While this can be time-consuming and ultimately better done via a dashboard, knowing you'll be asked about a task in a meeting does create an urgency to get it done. If you go this route, try to establish a routine of updating the status of action items in a dashboard or old meeting notes so you only need to review open items in the meeting. This is a perfect prework assignment. You can also remind team members to do this via chat, email, or a shared task management system.

CONNECT WITH KEY STAKEHOLDERS

There are often people who don't need to attend the meeting, but who still need to be informed of meeting outputs. As a meeting leader, it's your responsibility to ensure they are informed of decisions that impact them directly or will help them understand the context of their work.

As the priorities of your organization change, individual action plans must adapt accordingly. Be transparent about the latest updates and communicate shifting priorities with your team.

This helps the team to stay in sync. If priorities change, discuss with team members what the impact of changes on workloads would be. The same goes for each individual. As your personal workload shifts or a project evolves, be sure to communicate with your team if a task from a meeting is no longer relevant.

Sometimes individuals who are not in the meeting need to complete a task generated in the meeting. A good rule of thumb is never to assign a task to someone who isn't present without also assigning a person present to inform this third party. Never rely solely on sending meeting notes by email. If you need someone to take an action, reach out to her directly to ensure she knows what is needed by when and that she has the information she needs to deliver.

CHAPTER ELEVEN REVIEW

- Start meetings with a check-in to get everyone ready to participate. Choose the right kind of check-in for your group and purposes, and make sure it's on the agenda.

- Check-out at the end of the meeting to provide closure and allow for any final thoughts. Make sure this is on the agenda as well.

- Design activities for engagement, such as breaking into groups or using sticky notes to communicate ideas and to inject energy into the meeting. Also, use different voting methods to keep things interesting.

- All participants should be prepared to engage in the meeting conversation. If some need a little nudge beforehand, whether they are key decision makers or introverts, meet with them beforehand to make sure they come ready to share ideas.

- It's key to respect everyone's time. Start on time, end on time, and have norms in place regarding tardiness.

- Don't let the conversation stray too far off topic. There are questions you can ask and techniques you can employ to move things forward and keep everyone on track.

- Engage, even when you're not there. Let the meeting leader know your thoughts and that you're open to accepting tasks. Check in with him after the meeting.

- The meeting doesn't end when your allotted time is up. Engage participants after the meeting to ensure follow-through.

CHAPTER ELEVEN ACTION LIST

- As a meeting leader or facilitator, what are your biggest challenges in engaging meeting participants? List them on a piece of paper.
- Review all the engagement strategies in this chapter. Are any of them helpful for the challenge you're facing?
- If you were to try some engagement strategies, what are the top 1–2 things you'd like to implement in your next meeting?
- Visit the Resource section at the back of this book or online at www.meeteor.com/momentum/resources for additional check-in and check-out questions, and other engagement support.

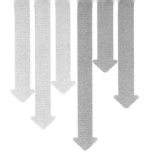

Chapter Twelve

Notes

———

The phrase "meeting notes" conjures a variety of images: scribbled key words in a notebook, a few bullet points in an email, a transcript of the "who said what." If you recall the comic from Chapter Three, little was documented from the meeting and the notes didn't accurately reflect the meeting's discussion.

One of the most overlooked problems with meetings is when the conversation is rich and productive, but the follow-through is lacking. I've been to numerous meetings like this, where the insufficient meeting notes mean people will need to spend time trying to figure out what was actually agreed upon and who should do what next.

These meetings are deceptive. There is great conversation. The group reaches agreement and enjoys the collaboration. You feel positive walking out of the meeting room. But a week later, your memory is blurry. Or, maybe it's your coworker who doesn't remember correctly. It's hard to know, because neither of you agree on the conclusions reached. So, in the next meeting, you find yourself debating with a team member about what the final decision was and who said she was going to do what. Without proper notes, it's a memory game no one wins. Instead of moving work forward, the team wastes time rehashing the same old conversation.

Almost no meeting should end without some form of notes. The process of creating the notes can vary, but having a shared record of the meeting is critical to the success of the meeting and to managing effective follow-through. Shared notes create transparency, which is key to developing trust within an organization. When anyone can access key materials, people feel like they can move forward with confidence because information is flowing clearly and seamlessly. Additionally, they don't need to attend a meeting to stay in the loop, enabling them to be more productive and selective with their time.

KEEP OTHERS INFORMED

Good meeting notes keep people who are not in the meeting informed in a way that's accessible and accurate. They can read key takeaways, know exactly what they need to know, and feel aligned with meeting participants. When you don't have shared meeting notes, you risk some key stakeholders not being informed or, worse, different people hearing different messages about the meeting outcomes.

One organization I worked with struggled with imbalanced information sharing. After their weekly team leadership meetings, each senior manager was asked to report back key takeaways to their department. Some managers did this regularly while others were inconsistent. It became problematic when individuals across different departments learned of initiatives and other decisions secondhand, and days or weeks later. It didn't engender a level of trust or respect between staff and supervisors, nor did it help people feel connected to the organization overall.

SAY NO TO MEETINGS

When you have a consistent note sharing practice, people at all levels of the organization can opt out of meetings without concern. This is especially powerful for people with decision-making authority but who don't necessarily have to be in every meeting. I love when my teams meet without me and send me the notes afterward. Rather than filling my day with meetings in which I'm not really needed and creating a culture in which I make all the decisions, I'm able to build trust and empower people to own their role. Within 24 hours of a meeting, typically sooner, I receive the meeting notes by email. In 30 seconds, I can see exactly what decisions were made and what the next steps are. If I have any concerns, I can jump right in, contact the meeting leader, and intervene. I'm usually in agreement with what they come up with on their own. This practice has helped each person take responsibility, while building a strong organizational culture that is not founder-dependent. I personally love it because each person gets to develop and grow without me, and I get my time back—yet I'm still completely in the loop.

MAKE A RECORD

Notes also serve as an historical record of the meeting. It can be painful to sit in a meeting discussing the same things over and over. "Why are we talking about this again?" you wonder. But you know the answer is because no one wrote down what we decided last time we discussed this topic, and everyone's forgotten what we agreed to. Or, just as bad, it was captured in a notebook or email or somewhere else, but trying to find those notes will take just as long as letting the conversation unfold for a second or third time.

When you have a record of the meeting, you can refer to the notes at various times. You can intervene in a discussion and point to the decision that was previously made, or remind a colleague he committed to a next step. If you have a new colleague or someone who's joining a team midway through a project, notes can be a great way to catch her up. By sending her the project's meeting notes, in a short time, she'll have a decent understanding of the history of the project.

They also can help guide external conversations. If a client doesn't remember exactly what was discussed at the last meeting or suddenly wants to alter the course of a project, you can refer to the notes to remind him of what was decided. You can say, "I want to take a step back for a moment. According to our last meeting notes, this is what we discussed and you agreed to. I see now you're telling me something different. I just want to check in and make sure this new direction is accurate." Using the notes as reference helps you gain clarification while using a light touch. Often, clients don't mean to make such changes. They truly just don't remember what was previously discussed or decided, and notes can help refresh them.

KEEP NOTES ACCESSIBLE

To make proper use of your notes, you need them to be organized and accessible. How you organize them is up to you. I've seen teams keep meeting notes by project in a shared folder. Others keep notes in a software system such as Basecamp or Evernote. Consider how you name the documents so you can find the one you're looking for quickly, and at the moment you need it. One team creates a single meeting notes document for each project. Every meeting, they add a new table at the top of the document with that meeting's date and take notes in the new table. Over time, the document accumulates all the notes for that project's meetings, making it easy to find any decision or other information in one place. To quickly jump to the relevant note, they use "Control + F" and can search for any term in the document.

Some meeting software makes meeting notes more accessible, both in search capability and in how you access them. Consider when you're most in need of referencing the notes. Will you be at a computer, using a tablet, or on your phone? If using a mobile device, a note-taking app might provide a faster, friendlier experience.

TYPES OF NOTES

Meeting notes are notoriously useless documents. No one wants to write them, and certainly no one looks forward to reading them. One reason notes can be so painful is the way the information is recorded. I've seen meeting notes that read like transcripts with, "Mamie suggested we consider using an outside vendor. Tai responded that she knew of a few good ones that she could reach out to." I've seen notes that are simple bullet points running the length of the page, making it impossible to distinguish what's important from what's not. I've seen notes that don't make sense to anyone who wasn't in the meeting and notes that don't make sense to anyone but the author, and everything in between.

The problem with most meeting notes is that they are not crystallized, organized, and prioritized in a way that makes them useful and actionable. The key to taking good notes is to use a framework of Tasks, Decisions, and Learnings.

1. TASKS

Tasks, or next steps, are the most common outputs of a meeting. The challenge with tasks is twofold: first, differentiating between "suggested" tasks and those that actually need to be done; and second, clarifying who will do the task by when.

You might be familiar with a conversation that goes something like this:

Sara: We really should get updated numbers from sales.

Dan: I was thinking we should check in with Kathy about what she's hearing from the market.

Franny: I spoke with Kathy last week, and she mentioned there was some energy about the pilots.

Dan: Let's compile all the information before making any decisions.

So, what exactly are the next steps? And who is going to do them? Unfortunately, this type of interaction happens all too frequently. In this scenario, both of the aforementioned problems exist. Will someone get the updated numbers from sales? Will someone follow up with Kathy to learn more? Will someone gather all of the information into one document and share it with the group? It's unclear which, if any, of these activities are critical. Even if everyone agreed that all three should happen, it's also unclear who will do them and by when.

"We" and "let's" get assigned many tasks in a meeting. When you record notes without clearly identifying what is an actual next step vs. a suggestion, no one is likely to take action. The purpose of capturing a note as a task is to ensure clarity around what needs to be done, and then to hold the person responsible accountable for follow-through after the meeting. To do this, a task must have three things: a precise description of what needs to be done, a single responsible party, and a due date.

The more specific the task, the easier it is to do and the more likely it will be done properly. Which numbers the group wants for "get the updated sales numbers" might be completely obvious to one person, but, for someone else, it may be highly ambiguous. It often depends on the people in the room and the exact topic of the conversation. If you have any concern the task could be done incorrectly, thereby wasting time, energy, and/or money, be more explicit in the task description.

A task owner is critical to ensuring follow-through. I recommend you always assign one owner, never more, to any task. Even when multiple people will be working on the task, it's essential that one person be ultimately responsible. This is a smart practice for all tasks, not just those assigned in meetings. Feel free to include a secondary supporter or contributor to the task, if needed.

Sadly, in most organizations, you can't rely on everyone to read the meeting notes to know exactly what's expected of them. If the task owner is not in the meeting, assign someone who is present the job of informing that person of the task and making sure he has all the necessary information to do it. This is true for both people who should have been in the meeting but missed it and those who are tangential to the work. In the case of requiring help from someone who is not on the team, I recommend assigning the task to a team member to be accountable for task communication and completion. For example, if the webinar team needs an updated graphic from the designer, assign one person on the team to communicate with the designer and bring the updated image to the team. In other words, "get updated image from the designer" is not a well-documented task.

The last element of a task is the due date. Providing a due date, even if somewhat arbitrary, helps the task owner prioritize this item according to his other to-dos. Tasks without due dates often go undone. A due date can be written in many forms: Feb. 7, 2017; next Tuesday; by our next meeting—any of these will do. The important thing is to include them.

2. DECISIONS

It might seem obvious to write down a decision that was made, yet we don't often capture exactly what the group agreed to. Consider this scenario:

Dan: I like the idea of making a recommendation to leadership and letting them decide how to proceed.

Kathy: I agree. We can lay out the options we've discussed and the sticking points we've run into.

Meg: I also like this approach because it doesn't require us to get everyone on board before taking it to leadership.

Dan: Great. Sounds like we've got a plan.

Once again, can you articulate exactly what the decision is? Is the group going to make a recommendation, provide options, or both? When you are forced to write the decision on paper, physically or digitally, you can't help but crystalize the decision and ensure exact agreement.

In addition to writing the decision, I recommend you include a rationale statement detailing why the decision was made. Articulating one or two key reasons why it was the best decision is important for providing context to people who missed the meeting.

For example, imagine you work at a company that always has an annual all-staff retreat. They've done it every year since you've been there, and it's one of your favorite times of year. During these retreats, you get to spend the day with colleagues you don't often see in person due to the dispersed geography of the company. Then, one year, the leadership team decides not to have an off-site retreat. You find out about this in the monthly leadership team meeting notes, which are sent to everyone in the organization as a way of sharing celebrations and other important news.

As someone who wasn't present in the meeting, you might find this decision to cancel the annual retreat confusing. You might even begin fuming inside and go knock on your manager's door to complain. Worst-case scenario, you might start spreading your negative emotions to your colleagues, saying how frustrating this is and insinuate that management doesn't care about us anymore. All of this could happen simply because you don't understand why the decision was made. Maybe it was canceled because the team is planning a bigger event for the fall and they need to conserve the budget. Maybe they want to repurpose the funds for investing in a new office space or updated conference room video equipment. It's hard to know when the only information you can read in the note is the decision and not the explanation.

Just having that extra bit of information as to why a decision was made goes a long way. It also helps to include a rationale for those times you want to revisit a decision because new information has arisen or a circumstance has changed. Understanding what triggered you to make the decision in the first place can help you determine when to modify it.

At Meeteor, we decided to start with an iPhone app and hold off on building an Android version. We made the decision to build one mobile app at a time in order to manage costs and develop learnings about our customer's mobile needs. On occasion, we'd get a request for an Android app. It could be tempting to change the plan and build an Android app in parallel, given the customer requests.

Yes, if enough customers were asking, we'd revisit the decision. We keep track of every request, and each time we get a new one we reflect on our decision. Instead of feeling pressure to build an Android app because another person asked, we look at the real reason we delayed the build: We don't have capacity to build two apps in parallel and we'll miss the opportunity to learn from the first set of mobile users to inform how we build the second mobile app. When you've recorded the decision and the rationale, you're able to revisit the decision with a sense of what's most important so you don't immediately let new information derail a decision.

3. LEARNINGS

Learnings can be big ideas, insights, or any information worth calling attention to, remembering, and sharing. You don't need to call them learnings. Some teams prefer the terms "take-aways" or "highlights." Regardless of what expression you choose, I recommend you differentiate between general notes (which we'll talk about more below) and those that are truly meaningful.

To identify a learning, it's helpful to understand each kind of content that can fall into this category. First are big ideas. These include ideas for the future you don't want to forget, as well as suggestions for how to improve going forward. These types of learnings often emerge during an after action review or period of reflection. They can also surface after reading a book or article or listening to a podcast. They can answer these questions:

- What did we learn along the way?
- What might we want to try in the future?
- What lessons do we take from this?

The second kind of learnings are insights. These learnings aren't always obvious, so you might not have them at every meeting. Insights are generated when people in the meeting connect dots and share "ah-has." For example, someone might notice every time a newsletter goes out to the subscriber base, there is a spike in customer support. Or, perhaps someone identified that you've had success with three types of buyers who all have the same pain point. These are astute observations you want to hold on to.

Learnings also can simply be points you want to call attention to in the notes. For example, a meeting participant might mention he spoke to ten different customers that week, and each expressed excitement about the company's new online ordering system. The comment is not a personal opinion, action, or decision. It's only information, but it merits documenting for the sake of sharing positive news with stakeholders who are reading the notes.

Because learnings are more ambiguous than other note types, it helps if someone in the meeting pinpoints them. Saying, "That's a good insight. Make sure we capture it," triggers the note-taker to add the information to the record as a learning.

You also can ask questions to generate learnings. Some options include:

- What is the takeaway from this?
- Is there a so what?
- What insights were gained?
- What do we need to extrapolate from all of this?

Learnings, like tasks and decisions, can occur outside of meetings too. Think of learnings as a way to build a knowledge-base for your team. Maybe someone read an interesting article on their lunch break. Maybe someone did research that can apply to future projects. Instead of relying on the person to mentally store this information until it's needed, encourage your colleagues to share their takeaways so everyone on the team can benefit. If these lessons are shared in a meeting, capture them as learnings. If they're shared outside a meeting, make a place where they can be documented and accessed by all.

4. GENERAL NOTES

General notes act like a placeholder for information without a clear home. The ideas are not important enough to be a learning, nor are they an actionable task or decision. It's up to each team to determine what constitutes a general note. Some like to record people's opinions or positions on issues. Some use this to document anecdotal information. General notes tend to provide context or flesh out the thinking, but they are not necessarily important enough to be useful after the meeting, other than to those who didn't participate but want the fullest picture possible about what was discussed. General notes are recorded for historical purposes and are there for anyone who's reading the notes and wants more information.

DIFFERENT WAYS TO CAPTURE NOTES

Note-taking is a huge responsibility, and there are many ways to do it depending on the culture and practicalities of your team and organization. The following are several options:

MEETING LEADER

A meeting leader can take notes, although this added task might be somewhat distracting from the primary job of keeping the meeting moving. It's hard to juggle multiple roles at once, but it can be done. If you're the meeting leader and official note-taker, try capturing key words or phrases during the conversation. Then, at the end of the meeting, use your scratch notes to form the full meeting notes.

You can also ask each person to write down his own next steps as the conversation unfolds. At the end of the meeting, have each person report out while you type them up.

DESIGNATED NOTE-TAKERS

One person in the group can be assigned the role, either on a regular or rotating basis. If one person is particularly adept at the task or enjoys it, he can do it more often than others. However, I recommend allowing all team members to try it at least once to get a good understanding of what's required of the role.

Many larger organizations include someone whose sole purpose in the meeting is to take notes. This is fine, provided the note-taker has enough understanding of the content to capture the important information, or the team or leader identifies essential information for the notes. Otherwise, you can end up with long, unhelpful notes. If you just want the entire meeting on record, arrange for an audio recording and have it transcribed.

For some teams, the note-taker is expected to capture key takeaways and also contribute to the content of the meeting. I've been in plenty of meetings where this is the case and, instead of the person balancing their roles as the note-taker and a participant, she sits quietly typing away without saying a word. This is unfortunate, as the meeting leader invited this person to do more than write notes, and yet she was unable to contribute meaningfully.

If you want someone who can create powerful, useful notes, empower that person to help facilitate the conversation. See Chapter Ten's section on the note-taker for additional ideas on how the note-taker can play a valuable role.

CAPTURING NOTES AS A TEAM DURING WRAP-UP

The easiest and most convenient way to take notes is for the team to build the meeting record together at the end of the meeting. As part of a final five minutes of wrap-up, ask the group to quickly highlight decisions, action items, and key takeaways, or learnings. It's a chance to summarize all the information from the meeting and make sure everyone is in line and satisfied with the final outcomes. Everyone should be able to walk out of the room confident in knowing what action they need to take.

When you collectively build the notes, you've removed pressure from the note-taker to analyzing the conversation and figuring out what is a task, decision, learning, or general note as the meeting is unfolding. It's fine to decide what's important at the end and organize things accordingly. A successful wrap-up ensures no one can leave the room asking, "Why did we have that meeting?" or, "So what am I doing next?" You know what outcomes you achieved and everyone is in alignment and feeling something of value was accomplished.

While generating the notes, have one person record them, preferably in a digital space (email, document, or app) rather than in handwritten form, so they can be instantly shared with whomever needs to be informed. This also works in settings where having laptops or phones out at the meetings is considered inappropriate. Only pull the laptop out during the last 5 minutes to type up notes when it's clear you're not being distracted by other work.

To facilitate the group note-taking approach, ask the participants the following questions:

- What are our next steps? Who will do what by when?
- What decisions did we make?
- Is there any information that people who are being informed of this meeting need to know?
- Is there anything that needs to be captured for historical purposes?

Be sure to consider the needs of other stakeholders. There might be critical information that isn't a decision or an action item, but should be in the notes. When using this approach, you might only have a few notes written down, which is fine provided they cover the critical takeaways of the meeting.

It's helpful for participants to know you'll be using this approach at the start of the meeting so they can keep track of thoughts along the way. Some teams ask each person to track their own tasks and then do a round-robin during the wrap-up so each person can share his next steps. You might also want to write down key phrases for decisions and learnings as they come up and flesh them out for the notes during the go around.

Keep in mind, this practice is not always ideal. For meetings that are more than an hour long, participants might forget critical information along the way. If you're having a decision-making meeting, you might want the notes to capture all alternatives considered, not just the final decision. You might want to know why the team voted against something, the pros and cons of each suggestion, and why the decision ultimately went the way it did.

In planning and producing meetings, you're often modifying or updating an existing document. You may only need to keep track of reasons for major changes because you're making the actual changes in real-time, directly into the material. Similarly, ideation meetings often involve writing on sticky notes, a white-board, or a flip chart, so you already have a record of the ideas. If you do use boards or other ways to capture thinking, take photos and circulate them with the notes.

The importance of note-taking in alignment meetings depends on who's present and who else needs to be informed. Connection meetings typically don't require notes unless they're for your own personal use. The need for detailed notes depends on the format of your meeting, who was present, and who else needs to be informed.

TAKE NOTES YOUR WAY

Take notes using whatever process works best for you. A lot of people still prefer to take handwritten notes. If you are one of them, use the last 5 minutes of the meeting to type up critical pieces of information. You don't have to type up all your notes at this point, just key takeaways. The goal is to leave the meeting having circulated the notes that are essential to work moving forward.

Regardless of your approach, you want to be sure the final product clearly articulates the tasks, decisions, and learnings in a format that helps others quickly grasp what they need to know.

SHARE NOTES TO MANAGE FOLLOW-THROUGH

As previously explained, the best way to guarantee that tasks discussed in the meeting come to fruition is to assign an owner and due date to each, document them in the meeting notes, and share those notes with everyone who needs to be informed. When action items are assigned to specific people, recorded in the notes, and shared for all to see, it creates a greater sense of accountability among the group. Anyone can and should revisit the notes from that meeting to see who is doing what and track completion.

SHARE BY EMAIL

Sharing notes can be as easy as sending an email immediately after the meeting. If you've captured notes in a document, send a link or attachment by email, but also include the tasks, decisions, and learnings in the body of the message. With the overwhelming amount of emails people receive, it's unwise to assume they will open any attachments, regardless of how easy it is. Plus, for those who search emails to find information, the search will only work if the content is in the email body.

HAVE A SYSTEM FOR STORING NOTES

One of the greatest challenges with meeting notes is finding them after the fact. Meeting notes get recorded in dozens of different places, and each person and team have their own practices. The more consistent your system, the easier it is to find notes to hold yourself and others accountable for meeting next steps.

There's no one way to keep track of meeting notes. Some practices that we've seen work well include the following:

- Create a centralized shared folder specifically for meeting notes. Create this file for each project or team you're working with.
- Use a meeting software specifically for note-taking.
- Attach meeting notes to the calendar event.
- Make a folder or tag in your email system for meeting notes.

COMMUNICATE WITHIN 24 HOURS

While it's best to have notes shared immediately after the meeting, that's not always possible. If you need to clean up your notes or obtain sign-offs from key people before sending them, aim to have a clean copy ready to share no longer than 24 hours after the meeting. If too much time goes by, you can run into problems that could have easily been avoided. Get people the information they require as quickly as possible so they can do their needed work.

This is especially true for individuals who didn't participate in the meeting. When my team shares notes from meetings I don't attend, I'm almost always happy with the results. However, I still want to know what's going on within a reasonable timeframe. If there's a concern, I need the chance to intervene as soon as possible. If days or weeks go by and I'm in the dark about an important decision or, worse, when I finally hear about it and don't agree with it, my trust in the team can be severely damaged.

When notes are not shared in a timely manner, you also risk wasting time and effort. If you are not in the meeting but are contributing to the project, there is no worse feeling than being told the work you've been doing is no longer relevant. Imagine if all week you were composing Tweets to help promote an upcoming workshop. Then, on Friday, a coworker tells you, "Oh, at our meeting on Monday, we decided to postpone the workshop due to low registration." How discouraged, angry, or resentful might you be? You would be beyond frustrated, and justifiably so. Not only did you waste time doing work that was meaningless, but clearly no one respects you enough to keep you informed. Meetings aren't always about starting new things; sometimes, they are about stopping old things. When people feel as if their work isn't being valued and they're not being informed, it feeds a negative team culture.

Remember, the great conversation we have in meetings is only part of the equation. While it can feel like its own accomplishment to have an enjoyable, rich discussion, the meeting's real purpose is to move work forward, and conversation alone cannot accomplish that. Meetings happen so next steps can occur. If you create tasks and they are never executed, or make decisions that aren't implemented, it can feel like a waste of everyone's time. You can avoid all of this by clearly documenting what was said and why, and who needs to do what by when.

CHAPTER TWELVE REVIEW

- Meeting notes perform several important functions: they can serve as a way to get everyone aligned, keep key players informed, and serve as a record.
- Notes must be accessible by everyone who needs the information. This helps everyone clearly understand why decisions were made, who is responsible for what, and creates an environment of transparency.
- The four types of notes are tasks, decisions, learnings, and general notes. Categorizing your notes in this way will help crystalize the conversation and make the notes actionable.
- Tasks must always have an owner and due date. Decisions should always be accompanied by a rationale. Learnings can be any information you want to highlight that others should know now or in the future.
- Bad notes use vague language and don't clearly communicate key takeaways. Good notes offer important details and provide all team members—including those not present at the meeting—a solid understanding of what they need to know.
- There are several ways to capture notes. Which approach you use depends on the culture of your organizations, the size of your group, and the reason for the meeting.
- Do a wrap-up at the end of your meeting to create alignment on tasks, decisions, and learnings.
- Notes are an effective tool for ensuring follow-through. Documenting who is expected to do what by when, and sharing the information with all involved, lets group members hold one another accountable.

CHAPTER TWELVE ACTION LIST

- Reflect on your current note-taking practice. Are your notes clear? Actionable? Referenced? Have you had moments when not sharing notes was an issue?
- What might be possible if there was a consistent, reliable note-taking practice in your team or organization? How would things be different?
- Try using the framework of "task, decision, learnings, general notes" to take notes at an upcoming meeting. Is this a practice that would benefit your team moving forward?
- Introduce the team note-taking approach at an upcoming meeting and try building your notes collectively at the end of the meeting.
- How might you improve your note-taking tools, sharing, and storage system? Pick 1–2 changes to experiment with. Consider using a software specifically designed to support effective note-taking.

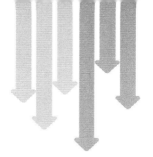

Chapter Thirteen

Technology

Technology is everywhere in our lives, and this is no less true when it comes to meetings. We currently have apps for managing your calendar (Outlook, Google Calendar), finding availabilities and scheduling (Doodle, Calendly), video and conference calls (WebEx, Zoom), taking notes (Google docs, Evernote, OneNote), and the list goes on! Despite the benefits these tools provide, they aren't always as user-friendly or reliable as we'd like them to be.

Everyone's relationship with technology is different, but regardless of whether you're a tech enthusiast or tech-hesitant, technology plays an important role in making your meetings more productive. Apps and software can impact all three phases of your meeting—before, during, and after—and using the appropriate technology can truly have an impact.

HOW MEETING-SPECIFIC SOFTWARE FACILITATES BEST PRACTICES

For decades, effective meeting leaders have followed the practices described in this book. They have been creating agendas and clarifying the purpose of their meetings, taking clear meeting notes and sharing them with key stakeholders, and following up on next steps to ensure they were completed. To support their healthy practices, they create agenda templates, bring printed agendas to the meeting, capture notes in a specific system, and transfer to-dos to their task list. They might use different tools, both digital and analog, or software to manage the various activities throughout the meeting cycle. As the workplace becomes more digitized and integrated, leaders need a seamless solution.

Meeting-specific software streamlines these tried-and-true practices, making it easier to incorporate them into your regular meeting habits. These tools provide structure, saving you time and brainpower and allowing you to focus on more important work. Apps for specifically managing meetings are designed to help you take the necessary steps to implement good practices and have productive meetings, ultimately enabling you to build and sustain a stronger, healthier company culture capable of achieving even greater results.

Earlier, in Chapter Three, I identified one of the key sources of meeting problems as the lack of shared standards for meetings. Using a meeting software can help establish consistent meeting practices across all your team meetings and throughout your organization. It doesn't matter who's planning the meeting or who's taking notes. Your team knows exactly what they can expect when viewing a meeting agenda and where they can find the decisions made in a past meeting. On an organizational level, meeting software fosters a healthy meeting culture by supporting consistency across different teams and departments.

TECHNOLOGY HELPS PLAN A THOUGHTFUL AGENDA

Planning a robust agenda can feel like a burden when you're typing it from scratch. You need to think about both the content and the structure of the agenda. Meeting management tools incorporate an agenda template so the meeting organizer no longer needs to remember the elements of a thoughtful agenda.

In addition, unlike a standard document template you create in Word or Google docs, a meeting management software is interactive and dynamic. It can provide contextual in-app help, such as examples and tips that help you craft a better agenda.

TECHNOLOGY HELPS TAKE NOTES

Unlike a typical word processor app, meeting specific tools that support note-taking allow you to easily create or tag notes as tasks and decisions. In some cases, when a note is marked as a specific type, additional specific fields will appear to help you capture all the relevant information that makes the note actionable. Once again, you no longer need to rely on the note-taker to ensure each task has an owner and due date because the system will prompt you to add them.

Tools that support this type of note-taking often also enable you to view the notes in various ways, such as all notes for a single meeting or all decisions recorded over the past three months. The content you've recorded becomes dynamic, making it easier to find what you need later on.

Most meeting management systems allow you to send a summary that organizes the notes so key stakeholders who didn't attend the meeting can quickly access critical information. The notes will appear both in the summary email and be accessible in the system.

TECHNOLOGY HELPS MANAGE FOLLOW-THROUGH

Robust meeting management tools support streamlined follow-through in addition to meeting planning and note-taking. The system becomes a centralized place for managing all your team's work.

These types of meeting tools include a full task manager so tasks from meetings instantly appear on the team's workplan and in the task owner's personal to-do list. This greatly reduces the effort needed to track accountability. Tasks assigned in meetings never fall through the cracks, and you no longer need to waste time copying tasks from meeting notes into your task system.

Decisions, learnings, and other notes become part of your team's knowledge base. For example, all decisions for a project can be viewed on a single page so they're easy to reference as needed. You can stop relying on memory or rehashing old conversations. Instead, view the list of decisions made or run a search to quickly find what you're looking for.

COLLABORATION AND COMMUNICATION TOOLS AREN'T ENOUGH

The spread of collaboration and communication tools has generally had a positive effect on meetings. Online chat apps that allow people to communicate quickly and informally have reduced email usage and meetings by providing an easier option for asynchronous communication. This has been particularly helpful for virtual teams. Slack, a popular chat app, says its users have an average of 25 percent fewer meetings, according to its 2015 customer study. Project management tools, task managers, and other online collaboration spaces allow teams to share information in real-time as the work progresses, reducing the need for status meetings. Document collaboration tools like Google docs and InVisionApp facilitate interactive feedback and questions on almost any material, without having to hold a meeting to review it together.

While the adoption of these tools has had a profound effect on how people work together, none of them address the root causes of unproductive meetings in a holistic way. Additionally, they all come with their own sets of challenges and limitations. The following sections expound the benefits and drawbacks of each type of tool:

ONLINE CHAT APPS

Slack, Hipchat, and other messaging tools allow people to share basic text messages and other media in chat threads on a given topic and with specific individuals.

Benefits:
- Enables quick and simple conversations, information sharing, asking questions without interrupting colleagues, and fun relationship building.
- Reduces various types of meetings and is ideal for identifying when a topic needs to move from chat into real-time meeting conversation.

Drawbacks:

- Can be frustrating when there are multiple conversations happening in a single stream.
- Often, conversations become long and unfocused with no clear outcomes.

PROJECT AND TASK MANAGEMENT TOOLS

Asana, Basecamp, Microsoft Project, and other task/project management tools allow teams to view and communicate about individual tasks and team progress.

Benefits:

- Helps teams keep track of and stay aligned on tasks and project timelines, connect conversations to specific tasks or issues, and find status updates without interrupting colleagues.
- Reduces status meetings and informal meetings to brief check-ins on specific issues.
- Provides context for big-picture meetings that can focus on goals and issues, which then are broken down into action items to be managed day-to-day.

Drawbacks:

- Can focus on the micro levels at the expense of macro issues.
- Only those following the tasks or project are informed and engaged.
- Does not facilitate problem solving or decision making.

COLLABORATIVE CONTENT PLATFORMS

Google Drive, Dropbox, InVisionApp, and other content collaboration apps allow for co-editing and/or commenting on given material.

Benefits:
- Contributors provide feedback on their own schedule, enabling them to reflect and respond when it works best for them.
- Often, more and richer input is shared because there is "space" for all voices and each person can take as much time as they want/need to respond. The group is no longer limited to one person speaking at a time within the time constraints of a meeting.
- Reduces presentation and feedback sessions. Ideal as pre-work for a collaborative working session with only decision makers (not all input providers) to resolve open issues on a document or work product.

Drawbacks:
- Can become unwieldy with excessive back-and-forth commentary.
- Often lacks clear process for making decisions when there's disagreement or multiple options.
- Ultimately, team collaboration software does support improved meetings, but they don't solve the fundamental problems of unproductive meetings. Use them for the value they bring, but don't expect them to solve all your meeting problems.

Introducing a new app that supports effective meetings can feel redundant or just plain overwhelming. Many people also feel a sense of app overload. A recent study by App Annie shows that on average, Americans use nine apps per day on their mobile device and thirty apps over the course of the month.

In addition to the stress of learning to use and manage dozens of apps, technology is often seen as a culprit rather than a friend. Despite the major investments and improvements in virtual meeting technologies, innumerable problems arise when using conference lines, connecting computers with the various adaptors, and screen sharing. These all create difficulties and frustration, which reduce the desire to use technology to support meetings.

Be aware of the tension between implementing software to change behavior and changing behavior then implementing software to sustain it. Tech-savvy people might look at software as a tool they can employ to drive them to act differently. Others might see software as a burden, making it harder for them to change because the best practices are conflated with using a software.

Each person and team are different. Before introducing any new software apps, consider what tools your team is already using and how these tools will interact with the new one. Can you replace an existing tool with a meeting app? Can you modify how you're using a current tool to make it more valuable for your meetings? You may find that the first step is optimizing your current tools, not introducing a new one.

VIRTUAL MEETINGS

With half of the US workforce currently working remotely, there are several important things to consider when conducting virtual meetings.

First, having the proper technology in place is key. When possible, opt for video conferencing rather than relying on audio alone. Video allows you to pick up body language and nonverbal cues, which help you better understand the speaker. It's closer to face-to-face interaction so everyone can connect in a more authentic way.

When you can't see one another, it can be hard to remember who is on the call, especially if it's a group that doesn't meet regularly. Instead of interacting with people, it can feel as if everyone is just a disembodied voice. Being able to see people humanizes them.

It's also harder to multitask when people can see you. You feel much more engaged because there's something and someone to look at. It's more obvious to the other participants when the conversation doesn't have your full attention. Peer pressure alone can make you stay focused so you contribute your best thinking to the meeting.

INVEST IN QUALITY TECHNOLOGY

For all these reasons, it's worth investing in a quality camera and conference phone. It can be problematic if five people are sitting around the table, but only those seated right next to the microphone are audible. Similarly, conference room cameras should have a wide-angle lens so everyone in the room is visible.

It's also important to choose the right video conferencing software for your team. Take the time to experiment and find the right platform for everyone's needs. If you have colleagues in multiple countries, you might find some conferencing apps work better than others.

Be sure to have a backup, should anything go wrong with your first choice. Our team typically meets by Skype, but if we're having trouble with it, we switch to Google Hangouts. Everyone knows it's our backup, so we don't have to waste any more time in our meeting deciding on a Plan B.

I was once on a conference call with 20 people and there was a terrible echo. The meeting leader kept saying, "Can everyone please make sure they're on mute?" The echo continued and finally became such a disturbance, the leader suggested we all hang up and call back in. Even after we rejoined, the echo persisted.

It turned out one of the people on the phone didn't know how to mute her phone. She had called in through her computer and phone but neither was on mute, hence the echo. She thought she was on mute until we realized it was her based on background noise. Someone asked, "Liz, are you on mute?" and she said, "I think so." The fact we all could hear her response proved she was not. Unfortunately, we wasted fifteen minutes of our hour-long meeting trying to get this echo to go away.

Minimize interruptions like these by making sure everyone has the information they need to use the technology appropriately. If needed, spend a few minutes walking a colleague through how to use the meeting tools. Include key instructions in your agenda, calendar invite, and reminder email.

CONSIDER CULTURAL DIFFERENCES

It's becoming more and more common to work with people across the globe. In these cases, it's crucial you are sensitive to the work style differences of people from other cultures and backgrounds.

It helps to set the tone from the beginning. You can use norms (see Chapter Nine) to help establish expectations and make sure everyone is informed of what is considered acceptable and encouraged behavior. What might seem normal to people of one culture may feel uncomfortable for people of another. There are many things you can do outside of meetings to help bridge these differences. Inside meetings, it starts with clarifying and advocating for the behaviors you desire.

Remember that, in addition to cultural differences, there could be language challenges. These can be exacerbated when you're meeting by phone instead of video or using poor technology. Some people speak very quickly or don't articulate well. This makes it hard enough to follow along, but then add that the listener can hardly hear the speaker who is sitting a few feet from the phone, or the video conference keeps freezing so they only get every few words.

It's important to build a team culture in which people are respectful of cultural differences and attentive to the complexities of working with a culturally diverse and geographically dispersed team. Encourage everyone to ask questions for clarification and speak up when they can't hear.

Finally, when scheduling meetings with people in different time zones, be sure to rotate times so no one is always stuck staying late or coming in early.

AMPLIFY WHAT YOU DO IN PERSON

Engaging virtual meeting participants starts by exaggerating what you already do for in-person meetings. When some people are co-located and others are joining remotely, it can be especially hard for virtual participants to jump into conversations. Make a note to periodically offer them the floor. If you go around the room, make sure any virtual participants are acknowledged as well.

Don't let multiple conversations happen at the same time. Side conversations, as well as papers shuffling or heavy typing, can be very distracting to those listening on the phone. Give the virtual participants the room's full attention and minimize anything that might be a disturbance to their engagement.

When using technology to connect, take advantage of what it has to offer. If using video, ask people to hold up their hands when voting. Set a norm that if you're having a hard time jumping into the conversation, type in the chat box to ask your question or say you'd like a turn.

If you're brainstorming, type ideas into a shared document so everyone can see them, rather than using sticky notes that only the in-person participants will be able to see. When looking through materials together, make sure everything is visible on the screen. Screen sharing lets everyone follow along together, regardless of how many locations are represented. Generally, this is easier than mentioning what slide number you're on each time someone gets lost. If screen sharing isn't an option, email everybody any presentation materials and be overly communicative about where you are.

Virtual meetings are here to stay. Technology isn't perfect, but good equipment and the right tools can make all the difference.

CHAPTER THIRTEEN REVIEW

- Take advantage of technology and make it work for you. There are many different kinds of meeting-specific software that can help enhance your meeting experience. Don't limit yourself to only using scheduling tools.
- Be aware of the pros and cons of using different technology offerings, and avoid app overload by sticking to only those that best serve your team and its needs.
- Having quality technology in place is especially key for virtual meetings. Make sure everyone knows how to use it to avoid unnecessary interruptions.
- Use video conferencing when possible so you can better engage with all participants. Make sure to acknowledge virtual participants just as you would those present in the room and give them ample opportunity to have their voices heard.
- Consider cultural differences when working with people in other countries. Be respectful of their ways of working, and keep time differences in mind when scheduling.

CHAPTER THIRTEEN ACTION LIST

- Think about how you can best introduce technology to make sure everyone is excited about a new tool.
- Consider what tools you're already using that could be optimized for meetings or replaced by a meeting software.
- Assess your meeting technology and equipment. Could you

invest in upgrades for any of these? How would this benefit your team?

- Determine what you think would be most helpful in a meeting software, e.g. structured meeting agenda, organized note-taking, ease of follow-through, access to shared meeting notes, etc. What tools or software might you experiment with? Check out ones we recommend at www.meeteor.com/momentum/resources.

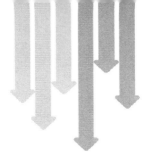

Creating Meeting Buy-In

The previous chapters are rich with ideas, approaches, and tools you can use to make your meetings better, but you can only do so much if your team is not on board. It's helpful to have a shared language and understanding of meeting practices. When you call out norms or desired outcomes of a meeting, you want your team to easily get what you mean. Managing the people side of change is the most important part of moving a team in a new direction.

GUIDE THE CHANGE PROCESS

Before I dive into the strategies to get buy-in from your team, let's go through a simple yet effective behavioral change model to give you a sense of why tools alone are insufficient for initiating and sustaining change. Developed by Jeffrey M. Hiatt, president of Prosci Research and founder of the Change Management Learning Center, the ADKAR model has helped tens of thousands of professionals implement meaningful change at their organizations. ADKAR stands for *Awareness, Desire, Knowledge, Ability,* and *Reinforcement.*

Awareness is about getting everyone on the same page regarding why change needs to happen. Once that occurs, you need to elicit the *Desire* to support the change, and equip the team with the *Knowledge* of how to implement it. Then, develop people's *Ability* to change by making sure they have the necessary skills and tools to do so, followed by offering *Reinforcement* that sustains this new way of doing things.

By reading this book, you're going through this personal thought process as well. The fact that you picked up the book proves you already have the *Awareness* that bad meetings are a problem in your workplace. The first three chapters lay out the details to enhance your awareness of the issue. Chapter Four then paints a picture of what successful meetings look like and how they can benefit you and your team. Hopefully, after having read those chapters, you have the *Desire* to take action to combat your meeting problems. This rest of this book offers *Knowledge* on how to implement effective meeting practices, and the action list at the end of each chapter is also a tool to help you develop your skills. Moving forward, it's on you to actually implement and incorporate what you learned in the book into your daily work. It's up to you and your team to *Reinforce* each other's behaviors.

Reinforcement is especially important at the beginning of any change effort, when people need to feel appreciated for work they are doing to support the changes. Team members should either reward or acknowledge the behavior to guarantee it continues. For example, you might say, "Mike, I acknowledge that you're playing devil's advocate. That's really helpful to our meeting because it makes us think from a different perspective." Such comments will help elicit the same desired behavior again in the future.

You can also celebrate outcomes to let the team know their efforts are not going unnoticed. In the above scenario, you might do this by saying, "I feel like we came to a really good decision because Mike played devil's advocate." Acknowledging the connection between the behavior and the improved outcome helps people realize the impact change can have.

MIND THE CURVES

While going through the stages of change, you will experience both an emotional curve and a learning curve. Pay attention to each as they are separate but interrelated.

THE EMOTIONAL CURVE

Everyone feels differently about change. You might respond with excitement because you love learning new things. You might be enthusiastic simply because you're fed up with how your meetings are run now and recognize the need for an upheaval. You might notice colleagues who dread or fear change. You might see team members who get anxious about change. All emotions are on the table when it comes to dealing with change.

I hope you feel excitement as you read this book. It's a great emotion to start with, but in most cases, you can expect it to wane at least somewhat once things get under way. Be prepared for new practices to possibly feel hard. There might be so much to learn and remember and do that the old ways start to seem not so bad. You may feel overwhelmed trying to champion the changes on your own. You might be tempted to abandon the change effort because it's too emotionally draining to be constantly running interference and reminding people of the new practices. But if you stick with it, the changes will begin to feel more normal, and you'll likely experience an upswing in excitement as they take hold and you see the results of your effort. Slowly, you will start feeling good about the improvements and become more confident. Then, you'll settle back into a new normal emotional stage.

Everyone perceives and engages in change in different ways, at different paces. For a person who's hesitant about change, you go through a similar emotional process but you begin from a place of resistance. When you start there, it can be even harder to reach the point of feeling normal again. Think about a ball that needs to make it up a hill. If it starts at the top of one hill and rolls down, it has some momentum to help push it up the next hill. If the ball starts halfway down the first hill, it has far less momentum to push it up. And if it starts in the valley, well, it may not make it up. It's harder to reach the new positive emotional peak if you're starting from a place of reluctance.

THE LEARNING CURVE

When it comes to learning, be patient with yourself and others. People learn in different ways and at different paces. Some skills may come easily to you and with more struggle to others. Some practices may take you dozens of attempts before they feel comfortable. If things seem difficult at first, rest assured knowing that the more you employ the new practices, the better you'll become at them. Over time, you won't have to think about them as much. They'll become habits and innate to how you function. You'll eventually reach a point where it doesn't feel like it's even necessarily a thoughtful, intentional practice because it's just become how you work.

Understanding your own transformational journey can help you introduce the changes to your team and the rest of the organization. If you can, be transparent about what's hard for you about the changes. Painting a picture that this is easy for you and everything is peachy will only make others feel inadequate and resist the changes even more. Let them see that change is hard but you're sticking with it because you believe in it.

IDENTIFY THE GAP AND CREATE A CASE FOR CHANGE

To initiate any change, you need to articulate what things are like now and what you want them to be. Scholars call this "current state" and "future state." Once you've identify these two states, you can pinpoint the gaps and plan accordingly. There is a natural tension between these two states. Peter Senge, one of the greatest influencers in business strategy, calls it the "creative tension." Imagine you're holding a rubber band with one hand pulling up and one hand pulling down. Your bottom hand is the current reality and your top hand the future vision. The tension on your rubber band needs to be relieved. You can do this in two ways: lower your vision and expect that less is possible, or, pull up current reality to make it meet the vision. There are many forces trying to pull your vision down, and I'll discuss how to mitigate them later in this chapter. For now, know that acknowledging this tension and holding strong to vision will help you make the case for change. Start by creating awareness of both the positive and negative aspects of meetings today and identifying where you'd like to be as a team or organization.

IDENTIFY THE CURRENT REALITY

The first step in any change process is acknowledging the existence of a problem. The goal in this step is to create awareness, introduce the concept of a change initiative, and engage people in the change process early so they feel more connected to the effort. This phase creates an opportunity for your team to talk openly and honestly about the challenges you experience. Is the problem a lack of planning or preparation? Does the team have difficulty staying on track? Does decision making seem overly burdensome and drawn out?

There are many reasons meetings can fail, so you'll want to pinpoint what they are for your team. Three ways to gather this information are:

- Send a survey, either anonymous or not, to all team members.
- Meet one-on-one with each person on the team and ask what they think about the meetings.
- Conduct a live brainstorm session in which you ask questions and give people time to write down their answers on sticky notes.

You can then compile the responses from the interviews and survey, or cloud-cluster the sticky notes to identify similar concepts. Then present the findings to the group to determine whether the themes that emerged resonate. No matter how you gather the data, the result is a baseline for your team's meeting culture.

A list of questions for reflection can be found at the end of this book in Resources and at www.meeteor.com/momentum/resources. Of course, you can also refer people to Chapter One of this book to select the pains that resonate with them.

ENVISION A BETTER FUTURE

Now you're ready to move on to the second step—what a better future looks like. Encourage the team to think about what they wish their meetings could be like and how achieving that vision would impact how they all work together. This helps people see how they can gain personally from change, which can generate more desire to participate in new practices.

As you did when identifying the problems, you can ask these questions through a survey, during individual interviews, or in a team meeting. Once you have the information, use it to connect the dots and determine which problems need to be addressed to create the kind of meetings the team wants.

If you prefer to tackle both the current reality and visioning in a single session, that's fine. Some teams find it helpful to separate them and really spend time focusing on each. Other teams prefer to work through them together in a single survey, interview, or meeting. There is no right way. You can also do a survey to kick off the problem identification, followed by a meeting in which you affirm the challenges and set the vision. Do what feels comfortable and manageable for your team.

A list of questions to spur visioning can be found in the Resources section at the back of this book and at www.meeteor. com/momentum/resources.

EDUCATE YOUR COLLEAGUES

After you and your team identify the current state, future state, and the gaps between them, you'll need to prioritize what's most crucial and determine what practices to implement. Thinking about the ADKAR model from earlier, at this point, your colleagues will hopefully have the *Awareness* and *Desire,* but may lack the *Knowledge*. There are a number of practices explained in this book that can help you bridge the gaps, but it's not likely everyone on your team will know about them. Consider the following approaches to build understanding of the practices:

- Provide a copy of this book to each person. Ask for commitment to read a chapter a week and, each week, discuss takeaways and reflections on what you learned during a team meeting.
- Share Meeteor blog articles or white papers with your team. For a recommended list visit www.meeteor.com/momentum/resources.
- Engage people to learn by doing. Introduce a practice at the start of a meeting and then use it. For example, write a desired outcome for the meeting. Spend a few minutes explaining what a desired outcome is and how you'll use it. Then assess your meeting at the end to see if you accomplished it.
- Connect with the Meeteor Team to lead a workshop, online training, webinar, or meeting transformation effort for your team or organization.

DESIGN YOUR SOLUTIONS

Once your team is familiar with the various practices and tools available, you can collectively determine which you'd like to implement. When making this decision, think about which approaches will be easiest to implement, which have garnered the most enthusiasm, which will make the most visible impact, and which will address the priority gaps you identified. There can be a lot of factors to consider, and you may want to be creative with your decision-making process. For example, start by listing changes and new practices the team is considering. Then, ask each person to rate each proposed change on a scale of 1-3, according to the previously listed criteria or any other criteria you like. Add up the totals and compare notes to see which practices fit the best.

I used this method with a team and the process itself was both engaging and illuminating. We were clearly aligned on some practices, while others were complete opposites. Practices I saw as being easy, others thought would be hard. The results allowed us to have a rich and focused conversation in which each person's perspective was valued and all the concerns were addressed.

If you prefer to introduce specific practices or tools you feel most appropriately fit your team's needs, go for it. Not every team has the patience to go through an in-depth process like the one previously described. But beware that there may be greater resistance if people feel the solutions are being thrust upon them. I recommend you start with practices that require less effort from the team to prove small wins and catalyze greater interest and willingness to try more practices.

FRAME CHANGE AS AN EXPERIMENT

Presenting plans for change as an experiment is one way to curb resistance. People are being asked to try something for a trial period rather than having a new way of doing things thrust upon them. When something is an experiment, it's automatically positioned for learning. The key is to frame the experiment in a way that builds commitment rather than gives permission to take the experiment less seriously. If people think they only have to get through a few weeks and then things will return to normal, they'll be less likely to put energy toward the change and participate with an open mind.

Explain that the goal is to improve some particular aspect of your meetings. The experiment is to determine whether this approach works to achieve that improvement and feels right and sustainable to the team. If, after a few weeks, the team decides it's not working, the plan is not to abandon the change effort but to make adjustments based on the learnings or experiment with another approach. The team is committing to solving a problem, not dedicated to one method.

For the experiment itself, suggest the entire group try a practice for a few weeks (or months, depending on your meeting schedule) then reassess. By assuring everyone there will be a period of assessment and adjustment, you help team members feel like they have ownership in the process. Don't forget to get actual agreement to go forward with the experiment. You want every person to verbally commit to putting their best effort forward.

Once the experiment phase is done, deliver on your promise to examine the impact. Ask the team if they feel their meetings have improved due to the new approach. Determine together whether there are any changes the team wants to make based on the prior weeks' experience. Depending on the answers, you can (1) call it a success and solidify this practice as a standard part of this team's work, and introduce a new approach to continue the change process; (2) modify the approach and try again for a few weeks; or (3) abandoned this practice and introduce a wholly new approach designed to tackle the same original problem.

This mentality starts to build a culture of continuous improvement. You're establishing a cycle of implementing one change at a time, evaluating it, modifying as needed, and implementing again. Trying too many things at once can feel overwhelming. Feathering them in over time allows everyone to adjust and accurately gauge effectiveness.

DETERMINE THE OPTIMAL APPROACH TO GET BUY-IN

Change efforts often fail because those affected are informed too late. If you're not involving everyone in the process of preparing for the change, they will feel bombarded and therefore less likely to show enthusiasm. Before you introduce any new practices to your organization, think about how you can set up the change process for success, starting with creating buy-in.

When it comes to making the case for change, people are motivated by different arguments. Some people will be inspired by the idea of creating a healthy workplace where people feel valued and engaged. They will intuitively understand the important role meetings can play in that.

Some people are more analytical. These people need to be persuaded by data, numbers, and statistics that prove the importance of a culture of effective meetings and the connection between meetings and results. They want to know how big the problem is and how much effort it's going to take to fix. They want to know about potential added costs and the impact on the bottom line.

Still others will be most triggered by stories. They will want to understand how other companies and teams successfully transformed their meetings and the impact it has had. Senior leaders may be moved by the "current reality" and "future vision" work you did with your team, helping them see the problem in their own organization.

Some will need to feel it for themselves. No amount of research or stories or data will convince them there is a problem worth addressing until they feel it. You may need to be creative in how you help these folks experience the current pains and future ideal. For example, a senior leader who never writes an agenda may not understand how challenging it can be to do so without a good template. Asking him to generate an agenda during your meeting could help him connect to the problem.

Yet others will require an understanding of the solutions. They'll completely agree with the problem, but be totally skeptical that any solution exists. Meetings have been so bad for so long, how could they be any other way? These people need to be educated on the fundamental practices of effective meetings.

Most likely, you'll incorporate elements of all these approaches into your pitch. Here are several ideas to help you build a business case:

- Share statistics and research on the amount of time spent in unproductive meetings, the importance of healthy company culture, and the problems with unproductive meetings.
- Include examples of how other teams or companies used the suggested new practices to achieve success. How you define success is up to you: greater productivity, increased employee retention, increased employee engagement, better bottom line, etc.
- Use a meeting calculator to estimate the time and dollar amount wasted in your meetings.
- Gather your own research on your team or organization's current state and future state.
- Provide a copy of this book to everyone who needs to buy in.

As you're putting together your case, think about the people you need to convince and decide what approach will work best in appealing to them.

For more information on all of these, visit our resources page at www.meeteor.com/momentum/resources.

ANTICIPATE RESISTANCE

Whenever there is change, resistance always follows. People resist for many reasons. Sometimes it happens out of fear of the unknown. Sometimes they're comfortable with the current state of things and don't feel the need to change. Perhaps they've had a previous bad experience with a failed or difficult change effort they'd rather not repeat. Some people see change as a personal attack on how they function. And some people are just slow to change no matter what. Regardless of the cause, you'll want to proactively plan for and respond to resistance.

ENGAGE THE RESISTERS

If you have a good idea who will be most resistant to implementing new meeting practices, talk to them ahead of time. By bringing them into the conversation earlier, you're able to better manage their reaction to and involvement with the change process.

Engaging someone early on extends the time they have to prepare for the change. Working with them one-on-one also prevents them from displaying their initial frustrations in front of other colleagues. Give them a chance to get any initial negativity out in a private setting where you can control who is exposed to it. This also gives you a chance to actively listen to their concerns. Of course, they'll likely still share their objections with others, but at least you've contained some of the initial emotional frustration and helped them to release it.

You also might ask the resistor to be the voice of the devil's advocate as changes are discussed. This way, you are giving him the job of being the person who is unhappy with the situation. By labeling it, your colleagues will see him as someone whose job it is to bring up counterpoints, rather than someone who is just frustrating or dragging the group down. Everyone will understand why one person is voicing so many concerns, and the naysayer now feels as if he is playing an important role, which changes his emotional connection to the project.

Sometimes you might not be sure who will be resistant to the change initiatives. Here, I've laid out some common reasons for resistance and how to best handle them. If you anticipate these reasons, you can address them ahead of time.

I Have No Idea What This All Means

People might resist because they are not aware of what the change entails. For example, they don't understand what counts as a meeting and are anxious about trying to apply changes to all types of conversation. This problem is about fear of the unknown and, for many people, the pain of the known is better than the potential of the unknown.

Combat this resistance by ensuring you have answers to common questions. Communicate the message clearly and engage the team to work together to figure out what is right for your team. Set definitions and boundaries as a group and explain the reasons for every action so everyone understands the importance of each practice. Use your own vision to frame how you develop tactics to help people feel control over the solution.

This Is Going to Be So Much Work

While the previous example was rooted in the fear of the unknown, this concern is all about fear of the potential. People understand what is going to happen, but have built up in their minds an unrealistic idea of what it will take. They see the process and effort as much larger and more complex than it will be.

The best way around this kind of thinking is to acknowledge it outright. Learning new ways of working does take time and energy, and people should not expect change to happen immediately. But the more they do it, the better and faster they will become at it and, eventually, the new practices will become familiar habits.

Don't minimize these concerns. If someone expresses worries about creating a desired outcome, don't say, "Oh, no, no. A desired outcome should only take you 2 minutes to write. It's a really fast thing to do, and if it's taking you more than 2 minutes, then you're doing it wrong." Instead, acknowledge that these practices probably will feel like they're taking a lot of time in the beginning, but that's okay because there will be savings on the backend. The few extra minutes spent preparing will result in fewer meetings down the line.

I Don't See How This Will Help Me

When everything feels too focused on the team, people can lose sight of how the changes can benefit them personally. Remind them of "what's in it for me." If the concern is, "This feels like it's going to be a lot of work for me to learn how to take notes so that other people can be informed," remind the person, "We all will benefit if there are good notes from the meeting. When you're out on vacation or you're home sick or you have a competing priority and you can't be here, it's going to be super helpful that someone on the team is going to have taken notes to support you staying informed." Help them understand why the work is worth it.

We're Already Invested in Another Change Effort

If your team or organization is implementing other organizational change efforts, it may seem like too much to also tackle meetings. In this case, flip the frame and position effective meeting practices as a driver of the existing culture change effort. As I described in Chapter Two, the interplay between meetings and culture is very strong. Culture is expressed in meetings. Therefore, if you implement the right meeting practices, it will impact and support the type of culture you desire.

For example, if your organization is implementing innovative ways of working, such as design thinking, introduce the idea of meeting norms as a tool to encourage innovative thinking (more in Chapter Nine). If your team is adopting the Agile or Lean Startup method, documenting decisions and key learnings can help you iterate your product or service faster. In this case, propose adding a wrap-up to the end of every meeting and suggest the task, decision, learnings, general notes method for note-taking. No matter whether you're restructuring to a flat organization, shifting to a remote workforce, or creating an inclusive environment, you can find meeting practices that support it. Effective meeting practices help move other initiatives along, because meetings are where a lot of collaboration happens.

Some people will resist change because it seems any time the company has ever tried something new, things revert to the old ways shortly after. It's the "flavor-of-the-month" fad that will quickly go away. There is no incentive to invest energy in something that will be obsolete in a few weeks. In such cases, leadership's support and commitment to the new way of doing things is critical.

To demonstrate support, you must be diligent about following through on your own commitments. Be a shining star role model and hold others accountable too. Treat this change effort as you would any other project or initiative and set a timeline, schedule meetings, and assign tasks to support implementation. If you take it seriously, others will too.

Additionally, employ any resources and approaches to change that specifically support sustainability, such as change champions and accountability partners. More on these to come.

LEVERAGE RESOURCES TO IMPLEMENT CHANGE

Once you've communicated the importance of changing meeting culture and started to manage resistance, find the resources that can help you sustain your change effort more effectively.

IDENTIFY YOUR ALLIES AND CHANGE CHAMPIONS

Who in your organization do people look up to when it comes to running effective meetings? Who on your team is open to new practices that can improve her productivity and quality of work life? Who in your organization has influence and will be aligned with championing or supporting your effort to change meeting culture? Are there leaders who are skilled with change and have successfully implemented other change efforts?

According to Bill Pasmore, Professor of Practice at Columbia University and author of *Leading Continuous Change*, as leaders and organizations successfully learn to implement change, they'll reach a "multiplier effect." Pasmore shares that when an organization is adapting quickly to stay competitive, the leaders learn about the process of change and can therefore better apply those learnings to other initiatives.

Find these people in your organization and talk to them. Share your plan and get their support. Leverage their influence or experience to get other people on board. Learn from them and have them share their stories to show the positive effects change can have when it's sustained.

ASSIGN ACCOUNTABILITY PARTNERS

Change sticks better when people are accountable to each other, and not just reliant on one person. Plus, you want the change effort to be owned by the team, not you alone. Assign or facilitate people in finding an accountability partner so they can help each other stick to the practices. For example, if the first change is coming prepared to meetings by having done the prework, pair people up so they can remind and check in on each other before the meeting. Having someone hold you accountable creates a sense of obligation. If you've agreed to meet your friend to go running twice a week, you're more likely to show up than if you've decided to run alone.

FIND RESOURCES FOR TRAINING AND SKILL-BUILDING

This book and the resources at www.meeteor.com/momentum/

resources are great starting points, but there are other sources and tools available. Some larger companies have human resources or organizational development professionals who can help you. They might be able to support you to manage the change effort and educate people on these practices. Or, maybe they can identify trainings to attend or workshops to bring in-house. Some companies may even have internal resources on effective meetings that you were previously unaware of.

There are other companies besides Meeteor that are helping create a world with more effective meetings. Some are doing research, writing articles, or producing how-to guides. Others are consultants and coaches working directly with clients. Some educational institutions and learning platforms offer classes online and off-line. Don't forget about technology tools as well. Some of these companies offer trainings on their software and the best practices they've built into their products.

CHANGE AS A TEAM IS MORE POWERFUL

You might think changing one person's behavior is hard enough, so changing a team's behavior must be even harder. On the contrary, research shows that changing behavior as a group can actually be more powerful. When we are doing something on our own, we tend to be more risk-averse and have fewer reinforcements. Groups create accountability and safety, so we're more committed to the change and willing to try something different.

DO WHAT YOU CAN

While making change as a team is ideal, not everyone is in a position to make that happen right away. If you, as the leader, think your team is not ready for the change, focus on the things you can control yourself. It's okay to start small. Begin by writing a desired outcome for each of your meetings. Introduce things slowly and draw attention to them. Tell the team, "You might have noticed I started sending a desired outcome for each meeting and then asking if we accomplished it as we conclude. I did this because I read a book and I thought we could make improvements to our meetings." Over time, you can add additional practices like assigning prework. Then, encourage the team to consider making better meetings a group effort. Even small changes you make yourself are a first step toward real change.

If you're not a meeting leader, there are still things you can do. Take it upon yourself to become the team's note-taker and share what you captured. Offer to play devil's advocate or capture off-topic ideas in a back burner. Everyone can do something to support more effective meetings.

Set yourself up for small wins to create a sense of success for the team. Don't start with larger changes that require participation from the entire group, such as implementing norms. Help them see the changes are worthwhile by pointing to the success of even the most basic new practices. Then, create momentum for additional changes requiring more people.

MEASURE THE IMPACT

In Chapter Three, I mentioned the ROI of implementing effective meeting practices is not easy to measure, but it's not impossible. Improvements that happen slowly are often not felt due to the incremental nature of change. It's like slowly boiling a frog. The frog doesn't notice the water getting hotter because it's only going up one degree at a time.

One way to help your team take notice of the improvements is to compare them with a baseline. Do a pre-assessment on your meetings before making any changes to your meeting practices. Capture people's emotions about meetings as well as their reflections on the current and future state (more on this earlier in this chapter).

Then, experiment with one or more practices for a period of time and reassess. Ask your team to quickly reflect on the effectiveness of your meetings. Compare these responses to the baseline you previously established and point out the differences.

For a more rigorous approach, you can measure the effectiveness of each meeting. As you do check-out, ask each person to do a Fist of 5 vote on how productive and worthwhile this meeting was. Keep track of those numbers and then look at the trends over time. Do people feel your meetings have gotten better as you've incorporated additional good practices?

It's also helpful to have a goal around meeting effectiveness. Try writing a SMART (specific, measurable, achievable, results-focused, and time-bound) goal that captures the improvement you seek. For example, "to reduce the collective time spent in meetings by 20 percent within 6 months" or "to enable a culture in which people can and do opt out of meetings without being left in the dark by March 1." This type of clarity will help the team determine what needs to be tracked to know if the goal was successfully met.

If you're undergoing an organization-wide effort, compare

your assessment results with other organizational health metrics, like employee engagement and retention.

If you hear stories and anecdotal evidence along the way, be sure to capture that too. Off-the-cuff remarks like these make for great testimonials.

SUSTAIN THE CHANGE

You've put in all the hard work to improve your meetings, so don't let up at the very end. One common misconception and cause of failed change efforts is the idea that once the changes are in place, your work is done. This is the *Reinforcement* phase of the ADKAR model. The phrase, "Get ready. Get set. Go. Keep going!" reflects the sentiment well.

Making sure changes becomes a permanent part of your culture requires ongoing attention. Make it a ritual to review your meetings once per quarter. Incorporate meeting preparedness and follow norms into your monthly one-on-ones. Check in with your team informally about your meeting practices, pains, and successes whenever a meeting ends early.

Any time a new member joins your team, introduce her to your meeting practices. Include specific actions, expectations, and language in your onboarding process.

And don't forget to celebrate success!

MAKE IT A HABIT—OR BREAK A BAD ONE

Another powerful way to sustain the change is to design actions as new habits. In his book *The Power of Habit*, Charles Duhigg shares MIT research that uncovers a neurological loop consisting of three parts—cue, routine, and reward—that forms the core of every habit. A cue triggers a pattern of routine behavior. The routine is reinforced by the reward so the next time the same cue occurs, the cycle repeats. When you want to build a new habit, connect it with an existing cue. When you want to break a bad habit, start by identifying the elements in the habit loop.

For example, let's say you attend every meeting to which you're invited, even if you don't really need to be there. Many of these meetings feel like a waste of time or are not relevant to your work. You leave most meetings feeling unhappy and resentful.

- Cue: The meeting invitation. Whether it's an email, a memo, or a phone call, the meeting invitation triggers your routine behavior.
- Routine: Click "going" and attend the meeting. You have not seriously considered the option of declining a meeting invite because you don't think your manager would approve or it's just "not done" at your place of work.
- Reward: You feel important, in the know, or like you did your job. You might spend the meeting time daydreaming, responding to emails, or stressing over other work you should be doing, but at least you're where everyone else is, staying informed, and doing what's expected of you. Plus, you've avoided the awkward conversation about why you didn't want to attend that meeting.

Accepting meeting invitations by default is an unexamined meeting habit in many organizations, even when the benefits of higher priority work far outweigh the benefits of attendance.

As Duhigg explains, the most effective way to shift a habit is not to change the cue or reward, but to focus on changing the routine. Next time you receive a meeting invitation (the cue), don't immediately click "going." Pause, and check the meeting agenda or details first (new routine). Then decide whether attending the meeting is the best use of your time. If there's no agenda available, reach out to the meeting leader to learn about the goal of the meeting, how you can best contribute to the conversation, or how to stay informed if you miss the meeting. This new routine yields the rewards of reclaimed time and reduced stress so you can focus on higher-priority work.

SUPPORT YOURSELF

Championing change is hard work. Give yourself space to reflect and recharge. If you feel like you're moving too fast, take a step back. It's not a failure if you pause on one practice in order to focus on another. Be transparent with your team so they understand the reprioritization and don't see it as a sign to give up on effective meetings.

Remember, you're not alone. There may be other people in your organization who are trying to improve meetings. There are communities online of people who are sharing best practices for implementing change. I highly encourage you to find a partner or a community, within or outside of your organization, to support you in the change effort.

Share with each other your wins, struggles, and learnings. You might find others are tackling similar issues that were also troubling you. You might see how your experience can inspire others to take actions. When you have a network of change champions who are dedicated to transforming culture, you are building the momentum to have more effective, engaging, and enjoyable meetings.

CHAPTER FOURTEEN REVIEW

- Managing the people side of change is crucial to ensuring success.
- Use the ADKAR approach to implement change: Awareness, Desire, Knowledge, Ability, and Reinforcement.
- Remember there is an emotional curve as well as a learning curve to any change process.
- When you make the case for change, consider the different ways people are motivated.
- Engage your team in the change process so they feel ownership over it. Let the team talk openly about why meetings are a problem and what they'd prefer to see happen. Decide together how you want to change.
- Framing change as an experiment is less intimidating to people.
- Resistance is going to happen. Have a game plan for dealing with it. Engage the resistors and figure out why they feel that way so you can best address their concerns. Engage team members who can act as champions of change.
- Celebrate successes, then sustain change by creating a culture where everyone is held accountable. Remember, change requires ongoing attention.

CHAPTER FOURTEEN ACTION LIST

- Assess your organization's readiness to change its meeting practices. Reference the Resource section and www.meeteor. com/momentum/resources for questions and additional materials.
- Identify the key stakeholders you need to engage in the process.
  - What's in it for them?
  - What are their concerns? What resistance do you anticipate?
  - What are your strategies to get their buy-in?
- Reflect on the ADKAR model, your key stakeholders, and the challenge of meetings in your organization. How might you create awareness, inspire desire, share knowledge, develop skills, and provide reinforcement?
- Create a plan for getting buy-in from your organization and choose the appropriate communication formats.
- Find the resources inside and outside your organization to support your change initiative.
  - Who in your organization is a role model for running effective meetings?
  - What resources can you use to develop the knowledge and skills of your team?
- Find the people who care about improving meeting culture to share practices and learnings and support each other.

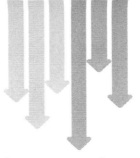

Chapter Fifteen

Frequently Asked Questions

At Meeteor, we get asked many insightful and revealing questions by thoughtful clients. Here are a few of the most common questions.

SHOULD WE HAVE WEEKLY STATUS OR TEAM MEETINGS?

Like many things in life, it depends. I suggest teams take a step back and question the reason they have these meetings. What do you hope to accomplish during these meetings? Do you want to build relationships and a sense of collegiality because this is the only time the full team gets together each week? Are you building a safety net to ensure everyone is aware of key activities across work streams, eliminating the chance for delays or miscommunications on timelines and activities? Or maybe you want to generate positive sentiment about the team and company overall, inspiring people to contribute their best work each week.

Once you know why you are having these meetings, you can determine the best format, frequency, and activities to reach that outcome. For example, if you want to build connection, perhaps a weekly lunch-and-learn in which team members take turns sharing or teaching about something they're knowledgeable or passionate about will be more effective. Alternatively, a daily stand-up might be better suited to work-stream alignment.

A meeting may well be the best format, but that doesn't mean it needs to be a painful, dreaded event. Think broadly and creatively, and experiment with potential options until you find the one that meets your needs.

WE'RE CONSIDERING IMPLEMENTING A NO-MEETING DAY, THE TWO-PIZZA RULE, STAND-UP MEETINGS, ETC. WHAT DO YOU THINK?

First, I applaud you for even considering doing something to tackle the problems you're having with meetings. Second, I suggest you reflect on whether any of these approaches will address the root causes of your problems.

In theory, fewer people are easier to manage in a room, people will be briefer with their remarks if you don't let them sit down, and you'll have fewer meetings if you force them into 4 days instead of 5. But, upon deeper inspection, you'll also see that including fewer people doesn't help if you're missing critical informants or decision makers. You risk participants not sharing their full thinking if they're tired of standing and just want the meeting to end. Meetings just don't stop happening or magically improve because you have one less day to hold them.

These tactics are popular because they are easy to implement and require minimal behavior change. Just like most quick fixes, the effort you put in is indicative of the value you'll get out. If you actually want to improve your meetings, try some of the other approaches we describe in this book.

PEOPLE ARE ALWAYS LATE TO MEETINGS. HOW CAN I GET THEM TO SHOW UP ON TIME?

Sadly, meeting tardiness is a fact of life and mostly for understandable reasons. It's currently impossible to move at the speed of light from your desk to the meeting room or to connect instantly to the conference line. With the intensity and overload of work most people have, it has become unreasonable to ask them to stop two minutes early so they have enough time to "relocate" to the meeting venue. Instead, people see the meeting starts at 9:00 a.m. and, at 9:00 a.m., they begin to make the switch.

This is especially true for more senior people and key decision makers who have back-to-back meetings all day. If they are in one part of the building for a meeting from 9:00 to 10:00 a.m., you cannot expect them to show up on time to your meeting three floors away at 10:00 a.m. on the dot.

I always assume my 10:00 a.m. meeting will actually start between 10:03 a.m. and 10:05 a.m. If everyone typically arrives at your meetings within 5 minutes of the set time, there's not much you can do to improve. Consider this good enough and stop worrying about picking up those extra few minutes.

If, on the other hand, someone is chronically more than 5 minutes late, it's time for a check-in. First, figure out whether the problem is related to something out of their control. You might discover Ben is regularly late to your Monday 2:00 p.m. staff meeting because he has another standing meeting right before that always runs late. In this case, either push your meeting back 15 minutes, find another time for your meeting, or speak with Ben about excusing himself at 2:00 p.m. from the earlier meeting, even if they're running over. He may or may not be able to do so. However, if Ben is late because he's not planning his day properly or for some other frivolous reason, it's time to intervene. Time management, which includes being able to show up to a meeting within an acceptable window, is an important professional and life skill.

Last, when someone is late, decide if you can start without them. If you can, do your best to not catch them up after they've joined. Unless it's a critical participant or senior leader, acknowledge the person's arrival but don't start the meeting over. Create a culture in your workplace where lateness is not accommodated or accepted.

For more on tackling tardiness, see Chapter Eleven on Engagement.

CAN I SAY NO TO A MEETING INVITE?

Yes, yes, you can. It might not feel right to do so, but that doesn't mean you need to let your workday be overrun with wasteful meetings.

Before you give an outright "no," be sure you understand the desired outcome of the meeting. If it hasn't yet been communicated, reach out to the meeting leader to learn more. If you know the desired outcome but aren't sure this meeting requires your presence, ask the meeting leader what value or perspective he hopes you'll bring. Why specifically did he invite you to this meeting?

If you agree you should participate, but still prefer to say no due to time constraints or competing priorities, speak with your manager. She's there to help you sort through sticky situations like these, where you have too much on your plate and need to figure out what can give a little. Alternatively, offer to contribute to the meeting in a less time-intensive way. Review the prework and send an email with your reflections, have a 10-minute check-in with the meeting leader to share your thoughts or ask what materials or information you can provide in your stead.

If you've decided to say no because the meeting isn't a good fit, don't just decline the invite without further explanation. Call, email, or chat with the meeting leader to let him know you won't be attending. Reiterate that if there is something he needs from you to help make the meeting productive, you're happy to help. If your culture requires it or it makes you feel more comfortable, be sure to clear all this with your supervisor first.

CAN I CANCEL A MEETING IF...

...I CAN'T THINK OF A PRODUCTIVE REASON TO MEET?

Yes! Many teams schedule standing meeting times or "landgrab" time on calendars months in advance to avoid the last-minute scheduling craze. While scheduling is a beast, we're usually good at getting meetings on the calendar. Unfortunately, we are not always so good about canceling meetings we don't need.

If there is no agenda, no desired outcome, and no one thinks the meeting needs to happen, cancel it. Consider the alternative: You will gather everyone into a room to accomplish nothing.

Along the same lines, sometimes you realize you simply don't need a real-time conversation. You might just share a report or an update, or have a few questions to ask by email or chat. There is no reason to hold a meeting for those types of needs.

Just because something is on your calendar doesn't mean you need to do it. If the meeting seems unnecessary, speak up. It's everyone's responsibility to make sure the time they spend together is not wasted.

As I said before, there's a reason the term is "cancellation"—it's "cancel" and "elation" combined. Remember, no one ever complains when a meeting gets canceled.

...NO ONE COMES PREPARED?

Possibly. Lack of preparation is a chronic issue in many organizations. You need to consider the importance of the work to be done in the meeting and whether you think the group can achieve the desired outcome, despite the inadequate readiness. If the meeting can wait, canceling it is a powerful message to the participants that you take meeting prework seriously. Be sure they know this isn't a moment to celebrate—a surprise extra hour at their desk—but rather a disappointment that you hope to avoid in the future.

...THERE IS NO AGENDA/PREWORK SENT AHEAD OF TIME?

If you have the authority to cancel or reschedule the meeting, yes! We've seen organizations and individuals with a strong practice of "no agenda, no meeting." They've determined an agenda is required if you want to have a productive meeting. If you've made it known that you expect an agenda 24 hours prior to any meetings you attend, you can consider canceling or rescheduling any that don't meet that standard.

This rule should be applied equally to your own meetings. If you are unable to produce and share an agenda for a scheduled meeting at least 24 hours in advance, hold yourself to the same standard and cancel or reschedule the meeting.

DOES EVERY MEETING NEED TO BE PLANNED IN ADVANCE?

The short answer is no. Obviously, when you have an impromptu meeting or urgent conversation, you won't have time to plan an agenda and send prework in advance. That doesn't mean you can skip following good meeting practices altogether. When you're in this situation, I still recommend you take a moment to get aligned on the desired outcome of the conversation with all the participants. You can quickly build the agenda together so you have a roadmap for your conversation.

You might also have regular check-in meetings with standing agenda topics that rarely change. In this case, sending an agenda in advance may not seem helpful because everyone already knows the plan. For these meetings, consider adding more detail to the agenda ahead of time or at the start of the meeting. For example, the two of us meet frequently to check in on the various projects and work streams we partner on. The agenda regularly looks something like this:

- Book
- Coaching
- Trainings
- Product
- Blog
- Other stuff

Before we jump in, we spend a minute specifying the subtopics and any decisions that need to be made for each. This way, we don't accidentally miss something or let the conversation wander on too long.

HOW DO I KEEP PEOPLE ENGAGED AND FOCUSED DURING A VIRTUAL MEETING?

It's never easier to multitask during a meeting than when it takes place by phone with 10 other people. Having the proper technology in place is key to the success of any virtual meeting. When possible, opt for video conferencing rather than relying on audio alone. Video provides an additional sensory engagement that helps people concentrate and creates greater pressure to stay focused, because fellow meeting participants can visually see when you're distracted.

If you do opt for video, encourage people who've dialed in to connect their phone to their computer log-in so when they're speaking, the group can see their faces. I've sat through way too many meetings where a black screen with a phone number takes over the main stage, while a thumbnail picture of the speaker is sidelined. In some systems, the meeting host can control whose video is largest, but this requires additional effort to manage and might not work for every team.

To help keep the energy up and engagement high, you need to pay extra attention to the way you conduct your meeting. For example, let people know you'll be doing a round-robin asking for thoughts so they'll listen carefully and be prepared to speak when you call their name. Try using a shared document during the meeting and having people brainstorm and write ideas or questions on the document. If it's a particularly large group, you might find it's helpful to use the chat box or hand raise features of the video conferencing app to ensure you don't miss anyone who is trying to jump in.

Much more on meeting engagement is in Chapter Eleven, and more on managing virtual meetings is in Chapter Thirteen: Technology.

HOW DO I GET PEOPLE TO PREPARE FOR MEETINGS?

It's inevitable you will have a few people who are slow to grasp the importance of prework, especially in the beginning. You may already be sending prework and have an unfortunate pattern of unpreparedness. Either way, the first thing you should do is check yourself:

- Is the prework you're sending clear? Does it include instructions?
- Have you set expectations appropriately? Do meeting participants understand the importance of prework and your intention that it be done every time?
- Are you sending an appropriate amount of prework? Is the format and content useful?

If you're sure you're doing all the right things, it may be time to speak with each person about their behavior or shift to a model of prework as the first 10 minutes of the meeting. To learn more about prework and how to get others to prepare, visit Chapter Eight.

HOW CAN I SUPPORT AN EFFECTIVE MEETING WHEN MY BOSS IS A "BIG PERSONALITY?"

You know your situation and colleagues best, but here are a few approaches to consider:

Speak to your boss privately about what you'd like to try and why. Be careful not to make poor meetings seem like a failure of her leadership. Instead, find messaging you believe will resonate most with her. Perhaps she'll get excited about being a pioneer of good meetings in your company or be willing to let you try whatever you want, as long as it doesn't require any effort from her.

During the meeting, you may need to be creative. If your boss is the one who always takes the conversation off topic, try reminding him of all the things you need to get through and how busy he is. You don't want to take up any more of his time than absolutely necessary. Or, if your boss is always carrying on and limiting participation from others, use an activity such as writing on sticky notes to get everyone's thinking down on paper. If your boss is also the meeting leader, you can request that approach for yourself by saying, "I have a lot of thoughts about this topic and I imagine others do too. I don't want to slow us down, so what do you think about spending two minutes writing our ideas down instead of sharing them aloud?"

Consider meeting without her. Do you really need this person in your meetings? Could you make a case that she skip the meeting and you'll do a follow-up with her about the meeting takeaways before implementing anything? Some supervisors may relish the idea that they can go to fewer meetings, while others may find it a total insult that you think they're not needed. Use your judgment.

Secretly (or not so secretly) leave a copy of this book on her desk. A gentle wake-up call may be all she needs to recognize how her own behaviors have been contributing to unproductive meetings.

For more suggestions on generating meeting buy-in, see Chapter Fourteen.

HOW DO I DEAL WITH DEVICES IN MY MEETINGS?

Many people are almost inseparable from their devices. To avoid distractions and multitasking, some meeting leaders are imposing rules banning technology in meetings. However, the problem is not technology itself, but how people are using it. Of course, you don't want people distracted by their email during a meeting, but some people prefer to use their phones to review agendas or take meeting notes.

It comes down to the behaviors you expect from meeting participants. If banning devices is intended to help people stay focused and engaged in the conversation, try using norms to address the unwanted behavior. "Be present and engage in conversation" and "use devices only to support your participation and engagement" are two norms you might consider.

Assess if anyone currently uses their device in ways that help them participate. If no one does, skip the norms and experiment with a no-device rule. One team we know of has everyone put their phones in the middle of the table at the start of the meeting. The leader ends the meeting at least 5 to 10 minutes early to give everyone a chance to check their email and notifications before heading off to their next meeting.

You need to hold each other accountable. For more suggestions on norms, see Chapter Nine.

HOW DO I COMBAT MEETING FOMO?

Step one is to acknowledge that FOMO (fear of missing out) is real and often has deep psychological roots. To combat your own meeting FOMO, separate out any emotional notions of meetings with the logistical ones. It's completely rational to fear missing out on a meeting if attending the meeting is the only way to know what's going on. When a team lacks transparency or basic trust in communicating key takeaways to critical stakeholders in a timely, consistent manner, you should be worried about being out of the loop. In these cases, make a point of checking in regularly with your supervisor or following up with the meeting leader after you've declined a meeting. You can even try asking a colleague to take notes to share with you.

If, on the other hand, your FOMO stems from the misguided notion that everyone should be invited to meetings or that meetings are a reflection of your importance at the organization, you've got some work to do internally. When you connect a portion of your self-worth to whether you get invited to meetings, you begin to fear being left out so badly that you want to go to every meeting just to be there. At the same time, you're just as frustrated as everyone else about how much time you waste and feel the same stress over losing valuable work time, and the terrible cycle continues. Identify this negative cycle and remind yourself that missing a meeting you didn't need to attend is actually a good thing most people would celebrate.

To help others combat FOMO, be sure to take clear, actionable notes and share them with people after the meeting. Be extra diligent in building trust with those colleagues who need to be informed but not participate in your meetings. Speak with them about the changes you're making to help create more effective meetings. Identify a few specific approaches you're implementing, including only inviting those who need to be in the conversation. Remind them you believe this will help them have more time to do their highest priority work and you'll do your best to keep them informed, but that at any point they can check in with you if they feel something isn't working.

HOW DO I MAKE SURE PEOPLE ARE FOLLOWING THROUGH?

Lack of follow-through happens for a number of reasons. Try to pinpoint the specific reasons people aren't following through and address them accordingly. Typical reasons include:

- Unclear next steps coming out of the meeting. Many task ideas get floated but, unless you agree to a next step, it's not going to get done.
- No assigned task owner. Even if the group agrees to a next step, if no one takes ownership, it won't get done. Don't assume anyone will take on extra work without being explicitly asked or assigned.
- No due date. Even with a clear, assigned task, without a due date, the task often falls to the bottom of someone's to-do list. Competing priorities and limited time means we tend to work on things with an impending deadline.
- Tasks from meetings never make it to the tasks list. Too often, tasks from meetings get buried in notebooks or digital meeting minutes. If you don't see the task on your to-do list, it's no surprise you'll forget to do it.
- No motivation to complete the task. While a deadline can create motivation, if you don't believe the task will make

any difference to the project, you're less likely to do it. It's important to only assign tasks that need to be done so they're taken seriously.

- No accountability. If no one is checking in and there's no negative recourse, natural or otherwise, why spend precious time on tasks assigned from meetings?

Once you've identified the issue inhibiting follow-through, you can take appropriate steps to address them. For more on managing follow-through, see Chapter Eleven: Engagement.

Conclusion

We hope the ideas put forth on the preceding pages have inspired you to make your meetings better. There is a great deal of information in this book, and, while you are hopefully feeling energized, you may also be feeling completely overwhelmed. You don't have to be an incredibly disciplined or detail-oriented person to do this. You just have to be committed. You don't have to do everything we suggest, nor do you have to do it all at once. You will almost certainly see improvement just by introducing one practice on its own.

The goal is not to do all the things you just learned. The goal is to improve your meetings. Some of these practices will work beautifully for you, others will feel like overkill. Some of them will be an obvious fit for your team, and others not work for your culture. Some will be met with enthusiasm from your colleagues, and others will be fought tooth and nail. Pick and choose which practices make the most sense to you. It's like doing yoga: You can do different variations depending on your own strength and capability. Do whatever you can to get closer to your goal of having more engaging, effective, and enjoyable meetings.

We also want to remind you that change takes time. You're in it for the long haul, so take things one step at a time, and start with low-hanging fruit to prove small wins. Think about where you have the most room to grow and where you think you will see the biggest impact. Is there something you can easily do to start down the path toward real improvement? Are there a few things you can do on your own before getting buy-in from others?

To help you plan, be thoughtful, and navigate the inevitable resistance, we've provided a series of questions in the Appendix and online at www.meeteor.com/momentum/resources. These questions will help you identify where your team already has solid practices and what areas need the most help. The questions will also guide you in determining what practices might be easiest to start with and how you'll go about introducing change, generating buy-in, and managing push back.

Some of these practices will become self-reinforcing. The more people do them, the more normal they will become. Some of the practices will require you to be intentional about them every time. Many norms tend to become habit eventually, whereas having an agenda is something you must deliberately do every single time. Even the most dedicated meeting planners, like us, occasionally feel the pull to procrastinate or skip crafting an agenda during a particularly busy time. An agenda doesn't just happen because you've done it a million times in the past. You still must make time to do it. You must continue to be diligent and intentional.

This is where accountability and commitment from the entire team become crucial. Holding each other accountable to the team's collectively shared practices keeps people from slipping back into old ways. It also ensures no one person is responsible for the success of your meetings. Everyone is in it together. Even as your team membership changes, a healthy meeting culture can continue. Psychologist Henry Cloud said, "A culture is like an immune system." It functions as a protection with the only goal of keeping things as they are. This makes changing a culture challenging, but once you've done it, it will take much less effort for new team members to become accustomed to these ways of working. That's what happens when a group is committed to a shared vision of productive meetings.

As you begin to see your meetings improve, don't forget to celebrate. Any improvement is worthy of recognition. If you do one small thing and see positive change as a result, acknowledge it. If you set a desired outcome and the group achieves it, say so. Show the team how one change led to a more productive conversation, and congratulate them on making it happen.

Remember, change is an ongoing process. There is no end to the journey, at which point you can say, "We have improved our meetings. We are now done." It requires constant attention and reflection. Always ask yourself and your team what you can do better. If the journey feels long and slow, that's okay—you are walking uphill, after all. You're always moving upward toward healthier, stronger, more productive meetings.

We hope you feel ready and confidant to make your meetings more effective, engaging, and enjoyable. We'd love to hear from you and help support you on this journey. Please reach out to us at book@meeteor.com with questions and challenges you're struggling with and stories of your successes.

To better meetings,

Mamie and Tai

Chapter Resources

___

CHAPTER SIX: DESIRED OUTCOME

EXAMPLES OF DESIRED OUTCOME

It's tempting to start a desired outcome with "to + verb." Here is a list of phrases to help shift your thinking to writing a desired outcome beginning with a noun.

- A list of...
- Agreement on...
- A decision on...
- Alignment on...
- Ideas for...
- Events scheduled...
- Stronger relationships among...
- Completed...
- Three to five questions for...
- Enhanced version of...
- Approval on...
- Answers to...

- Timeline set for...
- Clarity on...
- Next steps for...

In the two examples below, you'll see how the same content is shared with a casual and formal tone. Note that everything in [brackets] is meant to be replaced by your content.

Casual Style:

Subject: Tomorrow's meeting on [product spec priorities]

Body of email:

> *Hi all,*
> *I'm looking forward to our meeting [tomorrow at 9:00 a.m.] on [the new product spec priorities]. By the end of the meeting, my goal is to have [a final list of product specs to pass on to engineering]. Let me know if you have any questions.*
> *Looking forward!*
> *[Mamie]*

Formal Style:

Subject: Preparation for our meeting on [product spec priorities]

Body of the email:

Good morning.

In preparation for our meeting [tomorrow at 9:00 a.m.] on [the new product spec priorities], I want to be sure we're aligned on the meeting outcome. By the end of the meeting, we will have [agreement on a final list of product specs to pass on to engineering]. Please come prepared to engage in the conversation to help us achieve the outcome. Let me know if you have any questions.

Thanks,

[Mamie]

ASK FOR A DESIRED OUTCOME

Below are two examples of how to ask for a desired outcome using a casual and formal tone.

Casual Style:

Subject: Tomorrow's meeting on [product spec priorities]

Body of the email:

Hi [Tai],

I'm looking forward to our meeting [tomorrow] on [the new product spec priorities]. I want to be sure I'm prepared. I think the goal is to have [a final list of product specs to pass on to engineering]. Is that correct? If not, please let me know your thinking on what you hope to achieve during the meeting.

Thanks,

[Mamie]

Formal Style:

Subject: Preparation for our meeting on [product spec priorities]

Body of the email:

> *Good morning [Tai],*
>
> *In preparation for our meeting [tomorrow] on [the new product spec priorities], I want to be sure I'm aligned on the meeting outcome and ready to contribute to the conversation. It's my understanding that by the end of the meeting we will have [agreement on a final list of product specs to pass on to engineering]. Is that correct? If not, please let me know what you hope to achieve during the meeting.*
>
> *Thanks,*
>
> *[Mamie]*

CHAPTER EIGHT: PREWORK

PREWORK COMES IN MANY FORMS

Be creative about what you share as prework to make it useful and engaging. Here are some examples:

- Write a memo or document.
- Use bullet points, charts, and/or images to quickly get the idea across.
- Record a voice memo or video message.
- Write a case study that frames the background, context, and problem.
- Send a survey or questionnaire.

- Share an article, video, or podcast.
- Create an infographic.
- Ask people to reflect on specific questions.
- Ask participants to generate something ahead of time, such as a list of ideas.
- Ask people to respond to material and leave comments or edits in it.
- Ask people to gather information or data.

CHAPTER NINE: NORMS
GENERAL MEETING NORMS

Some norms refer to processes, preparation, and communication practices that can apply to any meeting. Below is a list of meeting norms we've collected over the years based on our experience facilitating and attending meetings. As you review them, consider which ones might enhance your team culture.

Process Norms

- We will respect everyone's time by starting and ending on time.
- If you enter late, feather yourself in without disturbing the conversation.
- Only one conversation at one time. Refrain from side talk.
- Capture off topic items in a back burner and agree to discuss them later, at a more appropriate time.
- Take bio breaks as needed. (Good for long meetings.)
- Everyone is responsible for helping to stay on topic. Speak up if you feel like we're getting off track.

- Everyone is responsible for upholding the norms. Acknowledge if you notice we are not doing so.
- Allow yourself to be facilitated.

Preparation Norms

- Be prepared and come ready to engage. Read the agenda and do any prework ahead of time.
- Come empowered to make commitments for your area or function.
- Put aside other topics and work so you're ready to focus on the discussion at hand.
- Meeting material and agenda must be sent 24 hours before a meeting.

Communication Norms

- Ask questions for clarification to help avoid making assumptions.
- Make sure everyone's voice is heard.
- Balance your participation—speak and listen.
- Listen actively to teammates without interrupting others.
- Clarify when you are advocating vs. offering an idea.
- Say it now, in the room. Avoid waiting until later to raise an issue.
- All voices count. All opinions are valid, but offer reasoning behind your thinking.
- Acknowledge when you're playing devil's advocate.
- Half-baked ideas are welcome.

- Our customers' opinions are more important than our own.
- Bring in data whenever possible.
- Be present with the people you are meeting with. Put away phones and other devices during the meeting.
- Only use devices if they support your participation.
- Challenge past assumptions and sacred cows.
- Address conflict head on.
- Look ahead to positive action, not back on shoulda, woulda, coulda.
- Aim for GETGO—good enough to go, not perfection.
- Ask "How might we...?"

NORMS FOR SPECIFIC TYPES OF MEETING CONVERSATION

There are many types of conversations that happen, and each will benefit from selecting norms that specifically relate to that type of discussion. Consider, for example, how a meeting might go differently if a brainstorm session has the norm "all ideas are good ideas" compared to "keep our resource constraints in mind."

Brainstorming Norms

- All ideas are good ideas.
- Think big and small.
- Build on the ideas of others. Use "Yes, and..."; avoid "No, but..."
- Defer judgment of ideas during brainstorming.
- Keep resource constraints in mind.
- Focus on thinking big picture (40,000 feet) or small changes (1,000 feet).

Staff Meeting/Check-In Meeting Norms

- Be concise and to the point.
- Be open to feedback.
- Share only new information, not a repeat of old information.
- Be sure your information is accurate.
- Acknowledge when you don't have an answer but will provide it after the meeting.
- Share celebrations and challenges alike.

Decision-Making Meeting Norms

- We will use [consensus, consultative, majority rule, fist of 5 voting] as our decision- making process.
- Each person is responsible for ensuring they understand the options and arguments before making the decision.
- Be willing to support a team consensus even if you initially don't agree with it.
- Don't push your ideas on the team after a decision has been made.
- Acknowledge when you are playing "devil's advocate" to help test a decision or idea.
- Separate your own personal feelings from what's best for the team/organization.
- Consider our principles/priorities/criteria over your preference.

Virtual Meetings Norms

Virtual teams have additional layers of complexity because not everyone is in the same room. Consider using norms that address the common behavioral challenges with virtual meetings.

- Don't multitask (do other work) during the meeting.
- Use the mute button at your site to prevent the transmission of background noise.
- Speak up to get attention if you have something to say.
- Use the chat panel to build the stack/signal when you want to speak.
- Turn on your video whenever possible.
- Follow an organized lineup to ensure each person has a chance to respond.

CHAPTER ELEVEN: ENGAGEMENT

SAMPLE CHECK-IN QUESTIONS

- Before we get started with the agenda, what's on everyone's mind?
- What do you want to mentally put aside so you can focus on this conversation?
- What's one word that can best describe how you 're feeling at this moment?
- How's everyone doing? (Or) How are you doing today?
- What's on your mind that you want to let go of?
- Anything you want to share with the group before we get into the meeting?
- What was your favorite movie as a kid?
- If you could meet any historical figure, who would it be?
- What is your spirit vegetable and why?
- What is one fun thing you did this past weekend?

- What else do you want to say before we totally wrap up?
- Do you have lingering thoughts or anything else you haven't yet shared?
- What's still on your mind that feels unsettled or unresolved?
- Any final thoughts?
- Are there any remaining questions, concerns, or unresolved issues?
- Are there any highlights or acknowledgments you want to share?
- How do you feel about what we achieved today?
- Did we cover everything we were planning to discuss in this meeting?
- Is everyone in agreement with the decisions made in the meeting? Is everyone clear about the next steps? Did we achieve our desired outcome(s)?
- How did we do as a team in this meeting?
- Did the process help us achieve the goal? If not, what can we do differently next time?
- How did the meeting go? What worked that we should do again?
- What are the things we can do better next time?
- What ideas do you have for things we could try doing next time?

CHAPTER FOURTEEN: BUY-IN

MEETING EFFECTIVENESS SURVEY

The following is a simple audit to help your team identify the current state of your meeting practices.

Select the appropriate rating for each of the following statements (1=strongly disagree, 2=disagree, 3=neutral, 4=agree, 5=strongly agree):

- The desired outcome of a meeting is clearly communicated prior to the meeting.
- The agenda for a meeting is shared prior to the meeting.
- I understand what I should do to prepare for the meeting.
- Every participant comes prepared for the meeting discussion.
- We refer to the agenda during the meeting.
- Participants are engaged in and contribute to the meeting conversation.
- I am comfortable sharing unpopular ideas or unpolished thoughts.
- I feel my perspective is valued and appreciated.
- Meeting conversation stays focused and on track.
- We assign meeting roles to participants.
- The meeting outputs (e.g. decisions, tasks, or next steps) are clear.
- Meeting notes/minutes are shared after a meeting.
- I feel like the entire team is on the same page after a meeting.
- We follow through on the tasks assigned at our meetings.
- I can easily access the outputs of a meeting (e.g.: decisions, tasks, or other critical information) after the meeting has ended.
- When I don't attend a meeting, I am informed of meeting outputs relevant to my work.

ADDITIONAL QUESTIONS TO ASSESS CURRENT STATE

The following questions can help guide the conversation:

- How much time do you spend in meetings each week? Is this time generally well spent?
- What do you think we do well in our meetings?
- What do you wish we did differently?
- Do you find our meetings to be engaging? Productive? Efficient? Enjoyable?
- Are there any meetings we have that:
    - you find are specifically well run or productive? Why?
    - you're not sure why we have them? Why?
    - you don't know why you're invited to them, or you don't feel are a good use of your time? Why?
    - could be replaced by another form of collaboration/communication?
- Have you ever declined a meeting for a reason other than a scheduling conflict? If not, why? What would need to happen to make you feel comfortable declining a meeting?

QUESTIONS TO GUIDE VISION

The following questions can help guide the conversation:
- How much more could my team accomplish if they had an extra day each week to accomplish their work?
- What would we gain if all team members felt empowered to share their thoughts in meetings?
- What would be different if everyone was engaged in the meeting conversation and no one was multitasking, daydreaming, or just sitting there doing nothing?
- What if great ideas were always recorded and we always knew where to find them?

- How much more could we accomplish if we all walked out of the meeting room knowing exactly what we needed to do next?
- How would meetings be different if everyone understood why they were there and came well prepared?
- What would be different if people who did not attend meetings were still informed of important outcomes?
- How would our team dynamic be different if people felt comfortable declining meetings or opting out of meetings when they had higher-priority work or felt their attendance was not vitally important?
- Think of a fantastic meeting you attended. What made it so great?
- What do the great meetings you've attended have in common? Have you worked with a skilled meeting leader? What did he or she do to make the meetings engaging, efficient, and productive?

ACTION PLANNING QUESTION LIST

The Action Checklists at the end of each chapter will help you reflect and implement actions specific to that chapter's content. The Action Planning Question List below will guide you through a thought process to create a plan for transforming your meetings and culture. For a more robust guide, visit www.meeteor.com/momentum/resources.

REFLECTION

- Reflect on your own experiences with meetings. What are some pain points?
- Envision your work life with better meeting practices. What does it look like?
- Among all the practices in the book, what practices would you personally implement today, this week, or this month?
- Interview a few colleagues about their experience with meetings and listen whole-heartedly. Be open to sharing your experience if they are willing to listen.

PLANNING FOR CHANGE

- What's your vision for the change? What does success look like for you?
- What's the scope of the change? Your own personal meeting practices, your team's, or your organization's?
- What's your role in introducing change? What influence do you have to make this happen?
- What are some meeting practices in this book you think will resonate with your team or organization?
- What is your organization currently doing? Has it provided training on effective meetings? Are there meeting tools, templates, and processes? Is there support for enacting changes to your meetings? If yes, what has worked and what hasn't?
- How might you create some quick wins? What are the low-hanging fruit?

COMMUNICATING THE NEED FOR CHANGE

- Has your organization, leadership, or team recognized the need for better meetings? Who are the key stakeholders you need to get on board? How might you get their buy-in?
- What resistance do you expect to encounter?
- How might you build a case for improving meetings? What stories, statistics, or evidence do you need to gather and present?
- How do you plan to present your case and introduce the concept of investing in your meetings (e.g. ask people to read this book, have a meeting about your meetings, write a case study, make a presentation)?

IMPLEMENTING CHANGE

- How will you determine which practices (e.g. desired outcomes, agenda, prework, norms, roles, engagement, technology) to introduce? Will you decide or will your team?
- How will you educate your team members on these practices?
- Who in your organization is a role model for running effective meetings?
- What resources are available to develop the knowledge and skills of your team members?
- What is your goal for improving your meetings? How will you measure success?
- How might you design an experiment around using effective meeting practices? How will you assess the impact?

SUSTAINING CHANGE

- How and when will you celebrate what you have achieved as a team?
- How might you build effective meetings into your routines (e.g. quarterly reviews, one-on-ones, onboarding process)?
- Have you found a community to support you in this work? How might you build one? Where can you look to find one?

References

Alban, D., 12 Effects of chronic stress on your brain. *Be Brain Fit*. Retrieved from https://bebrainfit.com/ effects-chronic-stress-brain/

Allen, J. A., Lehmann-Willenbrock, N., & Landowski, N. (2014). Paper 119. *Linking pre-meeting communication to meeting effectiveness*. Psychology Faculty Publications.

Allen, J. A., Lehmann-Willenbrock, N., & Rogelberg, S. (2015). *The Cambridge handbook of meeting science*. Cambridge University Press.

Cuddy, A. (2015). *Presence: Bringing your boldest self to your biggest challenges*. New York: Little, Brown and Company.

Detert, J. R. (2016, January). Can your employees really speak freely? *Harvard Business Review*, pp. 80–87.

Duhigg, C. (2012). *The power of habit: Why we do what we do in life and business.* New York: Random House.

Eddy, E., Tannenbaum, S. I., & Mathieu, J. E. (2013). Helping teams to help themselves: Comparing two team-led debriefing methods. *Personnel Psychology, 66,* 975–1008.

Gallup. (2015). *The state of the American manager: Analytics and advice for leaders.* Retrieved from http://www.gallup.com/services/182138/state-american-manager.aspx

Higginbottom, K. (2014). Workplace stress leads to less productive employees. *Forbes.* Retrieved from https://www.forbes.com/sites/karenhigginbottom/2014/09/11/workplace-stress-leads-to-less-productive-employees/

Kahneman, D. & Tversky, A. (1979). Intuitive prediction: Biases and corrective procedures. *TIMS Studies in Management Science, 12,* 313–327.

Kauffeld, S., & Lehmann-Willenbrock, N. (2012). Meetings matter: Effects of team meetings on team and organization success. *Small Group Research, 43,* 130–158. doi: 10.1177/1046496411429599

Kim, E. (2015, October 29). Slack, the $2.8 billion startup that wants to kill email, really is reducing work email. *Business Insider.* Retrieved from http://www.businessinsider.com/slack-survey-shows-it-reduces-work-email-2015-10

Mankins, M., Brahm, C., and Caimi, G. (2014, May). Your scarce resource. *Harvard Business Review*. Retrieved from https://hbr.org/2014/05/your-scarcest-resource

Maslow, A. H. (1966). *The psychology of science, a reconnaissance*. New York: Harper & Row, pp. 15.

Ohno, T. (2006). Ask 'why' five times about every matter. Retried from http://www.toyota-global.com/company/toyota_traditions/quality/mar_apr_2006.html

Pasmore, B. (2015). *Leading continuous change: Navigating churn in the real world*. San Francisco, CA: Berrett-Koehler Publishers.

Perez, S. (2017, May 4) Report: Smartphone owners are using 9 apps per day, 30 per month. *TechCrunch*. Retrieved from https://techcrunch.com/2017/05/04/report-smartphone-owners-are-using-9-apps-per-day-30-per-month/

Perlow, L. A., Hadley, C. N., & Eun, E. (2017, July). Stop the meeting madness. *Harvard Business Review*, 62–69.

Pothier, B. (2016). How running your meetings differently can transform your culture. *Inc.com*. Retrieved from https://www.inc.com/partners-in-leadership/4-ways-to-run-better-meetings-and-transform-your-culture.html

Rogelberg, S. G., Allen, J.A., Shanock, L., Scott, C. W., & Shuffler, M. (2010). Employee satisfaction with meetings: A contemporary facet of job satisfaction. *Human Resources Management, 49*, 149–172. doi:10.1002/hrm.20339

Schwarz, R. (2015, March). How to design an agenda for an effective meeting. *Harvard Business Review*. Retrieved from https://hbr.org/2015/03/how-to-design-an-agenda-for-an-effective-meeting

Scott, K. M. (2017). *Radical candor: How to be a kickass boss without losing your humanity*. New York: St. Martin's Press.

Senge, P. M. (1990). *The fifth discipline: The art and practice of the learning organization*. New York: Doubleday/Currency.

Suchman, A. L. & Williamson, P. R. (2007). Principles and practices of relationship-centered meetings. In *Relationship-centered administration: A sourcebook on transformational change in healthcare*. Rochester, NY: Relationship Centered Health Care.

Verizon Conferencing. (2003). Meetings in America. Retrieved 2016, from Verizon Conferencing: https://e-meetings.verizonbusiness.com/meetingsinamerica/pdf/MIA5.pdf

Acknowledgments

We would like to thank the many people who helped make this book possible. To the team of publishers, writers, editors, designers, and others who spent countless hours bringing this book to life, our deepest gratitude.

To our devoted team at Meeteor who has been on this journey with us to create a world in which more people experience productive, engaging meetings: Phil, Dan, Ezequiel, Botond, Alek, Lora, Mateja, Ivana, Sanja, Gordon, Lucija, Dorit, and Hoa. It's always a pleasure to be in meetings with you and learn from all our interactions.

To the Meeteor customers, blog readers, and collaborators who have generously shared stories of challenge and success. We consider it such a privilege to bring your learnings to the light.

To the leadership at GOJO, who recognized the importance of a strong, healthy meeting culture and did the hard work of making it a reality: Sharon, Barbara, Mike, Joe, Marcella, and Mark. You have taught Mamie and inspired her to make this her life's work.

To Tai's mentors for their guidance, support, and encouragement: David, Jessica, Bill, Stella, and many more great leaders, clients, and colleagues—thank you for being an inspiration.

To the thought leaders, subject matter experts, and researchers who laid the groundwork in changing organization's meeting culture. Your models, theories, and research have guided us to design, implement, and share culture change and meeting practices that actually work.

To our community and friends who have provided feedback, testimonials, and endorsements, your kindness and support fill our hearts and fuel our growth.

We also want to acknowledge each other, and the journey of co-creating this book. It's been an honor and blessing to have worked together and learned from each other.

On a personal note (from Mamie), thank you to my daughters, Syan and Briya, for giving up your mommy time to allow me to write on the weekends; and to my husband, Justin, for managing the kids and being my greatest fan. To my parents and siblings, thank you for your endless love.

Similarly (from Tai), thank you to my parents, for teaching me the joy of learning and giving back; to my sister, Melody, for always being my cheerleader; and to Angela, for your friendship and encouragement. To my partner in life, Yuxie, you're my rock, my love, and my best supporter. Thank you for always encouraging me to follow my dreams.

MAMIE AND TAI

BROOKLYN, NEW YORK

FALL 2017

Meet the Authors

MAMIE KANFER STEWART AND TAI TSAO are colleagues at Meeteor, a collaboration company on a mission to build strong healthy teams in which people thrive and organizations succeed. Since its founding in 2013, Meeteor has offered a variety of products and services to support effective meetings and teamwork, including web and mobile apps, training, consulting, coaching, and resource publication.

They believe in the power of effective meetings. When teams optimize their meetings, they unleash the potential for more joyful and effective collaboration. They know changing behavior is a complicated process. That's why they continually learn from their customers and evolve Meeteor's offerings to best serve teams and organizations as they adopt and sustain effective practices around meetings.

You can learn more about Meeteor and its services at www. meteor.com, or contact Mamie and Tai at info@meeteor.com.

MAMIE KANFER STEWART is CEO and founder of Meeteor. Mamie is passionate about helping others optimize their time and cultivate their team to achieve their goals. As a speaker and facilitator, Mamie has taught effective meeting practices at numerous conferences and workshops, including her keynote at Lean Startup Conference 2016. She has been a guest on numerous leadership and productivity podcasts, including The Productivityist. Mamie has been featured in *Forbes, Inc, Business Collective*, and *PCMag*, and writes about productivity, healthy team culture, and meeting best practices. You can learn more about Mamie's work at www. mamieks.com.

Prior to founding Meeteor, Mamie worked as a management consultant, helping nonprofit organizations with strategic planning, board development, and staffing. She graduated from New York University, Stern School of Business, and the Kansas City Art Institute. Mamie has served on numerous nonprofit boards and is currently Board Chair of Bend the Arc. In 2016, she was honored by Auburn Seminary with their prestigious Lives of Commitment Award.

Mamie enjoys rock climbing, trapezing, knitting, karaoke, and playing piano for group sing-alongs. She lives in Brooklyn with her husband and two children.

TAI TSAO is Meeteor's change management and customer success lead. Tai is driven to help individuals, teams, and organizations unlock their potential, transform the way they work, and make a greater impact. As a learner, facilitator, and change-maker, Tai brings the lens of learning, behavioral science, and organizational change to help teams be more successful integrating new ways of working and strengthening culture. At Meeteor, she develops content, programs, and learning materials to support the change adoption process, including strategies for incorporating new meeting practices, communicating vision, and evaluating effectiveness. You can find Tai's articles about improving meeting effectiveness and developing high performance teams on the Meeteor Blog, blog.meeteor.com. You can also learn more about Tai's work at www.taitsao.com.

Prior to joining Meeteor, Tai worked as a change management and organizational development consultant in a variety of settings: domestic and abroad, internal and external, business and non-profit organizations. She was also the founder of i Talent Learning Community, an organization that provides career development, skill building, and coaching programs for college students in Taiwan. Tai received her master's degree in social-organizational psychology from Columbia University and a bachelor's degree in banking from National Cheng Chi University.

When not working and learning to unlock human potential, Tai enjoys exploring cultural activities in New York City as a local tourist.

Printed in Great Britain
by Amazon